What Others Are Saying About
Planning Your Succession

" *Chand and Bronner provide a welcome message for times of transition and a needed message for times of stability. They truly understand that flocks must be prepared to survive the passing of a shepherd and that great leaders must develop the next generation. But the book offers more than important teachings on succession; it contains wisdom for everyone. Perhaps its most important message is that knowing the right thing to do is never enough; we must take action on our inspired knowledge and do the right thing.* "

— **Dr. Joe Astrachan**
Director of the Cox Family
Enterprise Center at
Kennesaw (Ga.) State University

" *This is not a book for those who just want to have their 15 minutes of fame. For those who understand that the greatness of what we build in life is determined by its longevity, however, it is a must-read.* "

— **Dr. A.R. Bernard**
President of the Council of Churches
of the City of New York and
Founding Pastor and CEO of
the Christian Cultural Center

"I greatly enjoyed reading this work by Drs. Chand and Bronner, as it teaches one how to flourish while enjoying the art of succession. It is no coincidence that the root word of 'succession' is 'success.' The exercise of succession will keep your family, religious center or business on a path of success. This book is a well written and thought out set of lessons and principles for anyone interested in improving themselves, their business and their families as they enjoy the passage of time. At the age of 64, I became more aware of my own behavior and my own future needs."

— **Dr. Joel A. Katz**
Entertainment Attorney,
Greenberg Traurig, LLP

"Planning Your Succession *is unbelievably clear, instructive and relevant. With this book, Dr. Bronner and Dr. Chand have given leaders a manual to create organizational success that lasts for generations, if applied. Whether you are a pastor, a CEO or even a mid-level manager, this book is for you. Offering their experience and expertise married with their personal integrity and honesty, these authors have produced a must-have resource for change agents worldwide.*"

— **Bishop Eddie L. Long**
Senior Pastor, New Birth
Missionary Baptist Church

"*Leaders are those who know the way, go the way and show the way. My friends, Sam and Dale, have created a must-read resource that shows the way for effective succession in churches, organizations and businesses. The seeds they sow in this practical book will benefit and secure a future for leaders and organizations!*"

— Dr. John C. Maxwell
Bestselling Author

"*Drs. Bronner and Chand make a very compelling, biblically-based case that the family-business owner, entrepreneur, and/or pastor has a moral responsibility to engage in serious succession planning so that their business or church organization will continue to be a blessing— both inside and outside the organization—when they are no longer involved. By challenging the reader to undertake appropriate succession planning—with probing questions and relevant anecdotes—this book will be a blessing to anyone who reads it and considers carefully its message. After spending many years, if not your entire working career, building your business or church organization, you owe it to yourself, to the members of your organization, and those to whom you serve, to engage in good succession planning.*"

— William J. Merritt, Esq.
Senior Partner of Merritt and Tenney Law Firm (Estate-planning attorney for the Bronner family)

"*Once again, Sam Chand and Dale Bronner have revealed another revelation, grasping a challenge and an exhortation often overlooked and more often undervalued. Combining their experiences in the sacred and secular communities, they address a topic of universal interest for every person who desires to leave an inheritance for their children's children. They challenge readers to take the concept of life and ministry to the next level with the thought-provoking question, 'How is legacy created?' More importantly, they help us to answer the related and critical question, 'How is legacy preserved?' They add a new perspective to the truth, 'Only what's done for Christ will last' and reveal clear pathways in that lasting direction.*"

— **Dr. Kenneth C. Ulmer**
President, The King's College and Seminary

Planning Your
SUCCESSION

Planning Your
SUCCESSION

PREPARING FOR THE FUTURE

Samuel R. Chand
Dale C. Bronner

HIGHLAND PARK, ILLINOIS

Printed in the United States of America

Published by:
Mall Publishing
641 Homewood Avenue
Highland Park, Illinois 60035
877.203.2453

Cover design by Worship Through the Arts, www.worshipthroughthearts.com

Book design by Saija Autrand, Faces Type & Design

Ghostwriter: Pat Russo, http://web.mac.com/pgrusso

ISBN 1-934165-24-7

Unless otherwise specified, all scripture references are from the King James Version.

For licensing / copyright information, for additional copies, or for use in
specialized settings, contact:

Dr. Samuel R. Chand
950 Eagles Landing Parkway, Suite 295
Stockbridge, GA 30281
www.samchand.com

Also by Samuel R. Chand

Failure:
The Womb of Success

Futuring:
Leading Your Church Into Tomorrow

Who's Holding Your Ladder?
Selecting Your Leaders—
Leadership's Most Critical Decision

Who Moved Your Ladder?
Your Next Bold Move

What's Shakin' Your Ladder?
15 Challenges *All* Leaders Face

Ladder*Shifts*:
New Realities, Rapid Change, Your Destiny

LadderFocus
Creating, Sustaining, and Enlarging Your Big Picture
(with Gerald Brooks)

For more information:
Samuel R. Chand Ministries
950 Eagles Landing Parkway
Suite 295
Stockbridge, GA 30281
www.samchand.com

Also by Dale C. Bronner

Pass the Baton:
The Miracle of Mentoring

Home Remedies:
God's Prescription for Your Family and Your Future

Treasure Your Silent Years

A Checkup From the Neck Up

Guard Your Gates!

Get A Grip!
How to Handle the Seven Toughest Problems of Life

For more information:
Word of Faith Family Worship Cathedral
212 Riverside Parkway
Austell, GA 30168
www.dalebronner.com

Contents

Foreword xv

Introduction 1

1. Succession Planning: Understanding the Need 3

2. Assessing the Avoidance Factors 15

3. Models for Succession Planning 27

4. Selecting and Developing Successors .51

5. Making a Graceful Exit 73

6. Considerations for Successors 85

References 93

Foreword

Chances are, you've heard plenty of announcers describe winning plays in major-league games. It's doubtful, however, that you've ever heard a sportscaster exclaim, "Hayford to Bauer to Tolle!" while reporting exciting play-by-play action.

Regardless of how hard I wish, there's just no way that "Hayford to Bauer to Tolle" will ever be as famous as "Tinker to Evers to Chance." Joe Tinker, Johnny Evers and Frank Chance are still major-league baseball's most famous double-play combination, nearly a century after the 1910 Chicago Cubs ran away with the National League championship. But I think I can confirm that the first trio of virtual unknowns discovered the benefit of transferring "the ball" in a way that resulted in multiple "wins," just as surely as the second legendary trio.

Some of you might question why I selected a baseball analogy to introduce a book on succession planning. When you examine the way the uncanny choreography, skill and timing of three guys can reduce potential losses and result in a win for the entire team, it seems a fitting comparison indeed. A closer look at the elements of a successful, winning transfer of the leadership "ball," from one leader to another further confirms its appropriateness. That's because the champions on any field never achieve success alone. Actual "wins" always require *a team mindset, a practiced pursuit, and an absence of preoccupation with who "looks best" or who "gets the credit."*

That's one reason it isn't surprising that this book is written by a team—Sam Chand and Dale Bronner. On this subject, I don't know that any pair is likely to approach these two, whose giftings and broad experience bring us the wealth of wisdom that these pages offer you. Both men are great servant-coaches who are dedicated to seeing others win. When those they serve do win, Sam and Dale won't be around clamoring for "the credit." They want *you* to succeed. Having tasted what can happen when solid succession occurs, I very much want you to succeed as well.

My first "taste" of successful succession came as a result of naming the first "trio" discussed above, when my leadership role passed to the two men who followed me. The effective succession we experienced confirms the principles Sam and Dale have distilled and provided here. I recalled much of what occurred to our leadership trio as I read the concepts shaped from their broad involvement and years of experience in transition with many churches and other organizations.

Scott Bauer and Jim Tolle were the two men who succeeded me, following my 30 years of leadership at The Church On The Way in Van Nuys, California. Scott took the helm first. Technically, Jim succeeded Scott, not me. But in a rather surprising act of providence, they *both* followed me into the lead role of service to the congregation. How did that happen?

It was almost an instant death. Four years into his remarkable success as senior pastor, an aneurysm burst suddenly in Scott's brain. In addition to the shockwaves created by his almost instant passing, the sudden departure of this dynamic, 49-year-old leader created many questions about the future. His leadership years were preceded by the three years he and I took to "pass the baton." Thankfully, Jim Tolle, an equally brilliant and gifted young man, had been discipled in the values and lifestyle of our congregation together with Scott. The second year after I left my role as lead pastor to found The King's Seminary, Jim became Scott's primary partner in leading the congregation.

Obviously, no one anticipated the need for such a sudden transition so early in Scott's tenure. The congregation's elders invited me to partner with them by serving as interim pastor for a year. During this time, we united in a prayerful and patient succession process, resulting in Jim's selection as senior pastor. Because of our application of biblical wisdom, much practical planning and an emphasis on relational values, our "succession of successions" was transformed into a God-given "progression of progressions."

The results of this planning are evident in The Church On The Way. During my three decades of leadership, the congregation grew from 18 people to more than 10,000. During Scott's relatively short term of service, it increased by another 3,000. Under Jim's leadership, it hit the 18,000-member mark, with an average weekend attendance of more than 11,000—nearly doubling in the ten years since I left. Numbers alone never tell the whole story. Our pragmatic planning and sensible processing provided a foundation for spiritual and relational strength in the congregation, qualities that continue to be a joy to observe. As the founding pastor, it's these godly qualities that cause me to rejoice.

Full credit for our report belongs to God alone. We give glory to Him and the wisdom inherent in His ways. You can rest assured, however, of the necessity of appropriate preparation. Divine blessing always attends wise planning, as humble leaders without private agendas allow the Holy Spirit's presence, seeking God's ways and inviting the wisdom of "many counselors."

I'm so pleased to introduce this pair of excellent counselors. In these pages, they present a wealth of pragmatic thinking and proven processes that will enable much effective succession planning. In commending them and their work, I've also offered my testimony to the blessings available from good succession. I conclude by punctuating my endorsement with two affirmations:

- Good counsel is *in your hands,* as Sam and Dale are *right here.* Ye, even more,
- Divine grace is always *at hand* because God is *ever near.*

Employ both sources; it's a sure "win."

— Jack W. Hayford
President, International Foursquare Churches; Chancellor, The King's College and Seminary

Introduction

Succession is "the thorniest, most dreaded, and least-talked-about rite of passage in Corporate America," said a recent *Fortune* magazine article.[1]

Like much of what's written about succession planning, this description provides an incomplete picture, treating succession as though it was only about filling current or anticipated top-level leadership vacancies.

> **Succession is not about filling leadership vacancies; it's about creating an organization's future.**

Succession is not about filling leadership vacancies; it's about creating an organization's future. It's about looking down the road, determining what future challenges await the organization and providing what's needed to arrive at the desired destination—including the necessary leadership. It should be a positive process, not merely a negative one.

If you're at the helm of an organization—regardless of your age—you should be giving more thought to your succession. Admittedly, that's a tough task for a leader who's between 20 and 40 years of age. If you're young and healthy, and your organization is vibrant,

1

it's easy to relegate thoughts of succession planning to the back burner.

Why make time for succession planning when you're young, when you have so many other pressing concerns? Because devoting time to leadership succession offers your organization tremendous advantages. By training yourself to think decades ahead, you'll build a much more solid foundation for your organization. You'll create your organizational legacy by design, rather than by default. And you'll equip it with the leadership continuity that's a critical component of any strategic future.

> **Create your organizational legacy by design, rather than by default.**

None of us is immortal. Regardless of our current age, we all need to give thought to how our organization will be guided without us. It's really not about us. It's about ensuring the healthy survival and prosperity of our organization's vision and mission. It's about creating a legacy. It's about being a blessing to future generations.

It's also about heeding the advice of Proverbs 22:3, "A prudent person foresees danger and takes precautions. The simpleton goes blindly on and suffers the consequences."[2]

Succession Planning: Understanding the Need

For months, President James Garfield hung between life and death.

While standing at a railway station in Washington, D.C., on July 2, 1881, Garfield was shot twice in the back by an unhappy political appointee. While the president fought for his life, his cabinet debated who would run the country.

Although the Presidential Succession Act of 1792 made it clear that the vice president would assume the office upon the president's death, it was unclear about what to do when he was incapacitated. Should Vice President Chester Arthur fill in as acting president, they wondered? Should he assume the office of president? If he did, what would happen if Garfield recovered?

For eleven weeks, the country remained leaderless, with no one paying much attention to the daily workings of the government. Upon Garfield's death on September 19, Vice President Chester Arthur came out of seclusion and became America's 21st president.

Two constitutional amendments and a 1947 law subsequently repaired the gaps in the country's succession plan. As a result, when

President George Bush underwent a medical procedure in 2006, Vice President Dick Cheney became acting president, with power passing effortlessly back to the president once he recovered.

Monarchies around the globe also have clear lines of succession. In each case, they provide an ordered list of the descendants who are next in line for the throne. Similarly, five vice presidents have assumed the presidency between 1901 and 1974 because of death or resignation. U.S. law also describes the order in which the Speaker of the House and the Secretary of State would step into the nation's top leadership vacancies.

Clearly, a nation's leadership is vital; its succession plan cannot be unclear or shrouded in secrecy. What has become a common policy for sovereign nations should also be standard practice for its corporations, its family-owned businesses, its churches and its many vital organizations. Unfortunately, that's far from the case. A large percentage of these organizations would be just as adrift as America was after President Garfield was shot.

> **CEO succession in the world's largest companies is 70 percent higher than it was 10 years ago.**

Consider the following facts:

- One recent study—which benchmarked public and private companies with more than 1,000 employees—found that 46 percent have no systematic process for succession planning. And 78 percent reported that they find it very difficult to find qualified candidates for leadership positions[3].
- Fifty-eight percent of small-business owners cite inadequate succession planning as the biggest threat that they're facing[4].
- Thirty percent of family-owned businesses are not considering their succession planning needs[5].

- Only one percent of the 18 million family-owned businesses in the U.S. are expected to be family-run into a third generation[6].
- Three of every four non-profit organizations—including churches—have no executive succession plan; less than four in 10 reported that they'd be creating a plan[7].

In our work with many large churches around the world, we estimate that 90 percent of the pastors that we speak with have no idea what will happen to their congregations when they die or retire.

With the Baby Boomer generation rapidly approaching retirement age, many experts are worried. Some fear that the talent pool that follows this generation is not large enough or skilled enough to fill the gaps. Those gaps may soon become apparent. Already, CEO succession in the world's largest companies is 70 percent higher than it was 10 years ago[8].

A lack of succession planning can be disastrous. When Frank Lanza died suddenly, there was no one named to succeed him as CEO of L-3 Communications, one of the country's largest aerospace and defense contractors. The company's stock reacted, shareholders complained, and *The Wall Street Journal* speculated that the enterprise was vulnerable to a takeover.

> **Succession planning creates a *leadership culture* within the organization.**

Contrast that situation with the successful executive transitions at General Electric, Microsoft, Ford and many other smaller firms. When fast-food giant McDonald's unexpectedly lost two CEOs in the same year, for example, the corporation lost none of its forward motion. These transitions were successful because they were well-planned and well-executed.

Benefits of Succession Planning

The value of good succession planning cannot be underestimated.

When implemented properly, succession planning creates a *leadership culture* within the organization. A true leadership culture is one that identifies and develops people who are able to function across an organization, who are cross-trained in a variety of responsibilities, and are ready to adapt to a new role with competence and confidence.

Don't assume that succession planning should be limited to the executive suite. An effective succession plan includes transition strategies for leaders, for managers and their direct reports, and for the valuable skilled workers at every level within an organization. By creating a succession plan that includes these key employees, you ensure that the organization will continue the work that generates revenue, satisfies customers and stakeholders, and remains healthy.

In family-run businesses, a succession plan can help ensure that everyone's opinions are heard and their needs met. In addition to heading off squabbles, having the family's buy-in well in advance of an untimely death or catastrophe may be enough to keep the company afloat through a difficult period.

> **A good succession plan ensures that your wisdom and knowledge transcend the current generation.**

A family-run business with a sound succession plan can also provide survivors with significant tax savings. If an owner dies without a succession plan, tax liabilities and estate settlement costs could comprise up to 60 percent of the assets.[9] The family might be compelled to sell the business just to pay the resulting estate tax bill.

Preparing your organization for future leadership transitions can also bring benefits today. It ensures that leaders and managers at all levels remain in synch with company goals, have defined career paths and developmental opportunities, and prepares you to respond effectively when key employees leave unexpectedly.

In addition to developing leaders, a good succession plan ensures that your wisdom and knowledge transcend the current generation. After the founder's death, some organizations change so significantly that the person who started the company probably wouldn't recognize them. The leader of one successful Dallas-based foundation put it this way, "I don't know any foundation, including our own, where the values of the grantor(s) are carried out in the third generation."

> **Before we can think about reproducing successors externally, our bodies are at work reproducing internally.**

As this quote suggests, there are simply too many cases of wisdom that dies with a company's founder. This happens in business, in ministry and in government, whenever we are unable to build on the foundation from the previous generation.

For a founder or an entrepreneur, a succession plan can provide the flexibility needed to explore other options, pursue dreams or develop other businesses. When Bill Gates resigned his day-to-day responsibilities at Microsoft, it enabled him to become a full-time philanthropist with his own foundation.

With a succession plan in place, an organization is also primed to take advantage of change. Having leaders who are prepared can relieve the stress of unanticipated marketplace variations and turn them into opportunities for advancing the organization. This expectant and confident attitude can have a ripple effect throughout the organization, energizing and mobilizing people at all levels, which can have a dynamic effect on future success.

Dissecting Succession

Healthy organizations have much in common with healthy human bodies. When God created our bodies, he created them with many internal systems. We have a reproductive system built to create future generations. We have a circulatory system that keeps energy flowing throughout our bodies. We have a respiratory system that receives life from the atmosphere every time that we breathe.

These systems are interdependent and innately regenerative. Our nervous system sends signals that start the movements that enable us to eat, which mobilizes our digestive system to produce energy from food. Before we can think about reproducing successors externally, our bodies are at work reproducing internally. If each system within the body does not keep regenerating itself at the cellular level, the entire system begins to deteriorate. The cells in our bone marrow are programmed to produce new cells.

> **We must value our organizations enough to develop other leaders into successors.**

This entire interdependent system is harmonious. If we break a toe, our bodies are so marvelously made that extra calcium from an arm is transferred into the cardiovascular system to begin fortifying that broken toe and begin healing. All of our other toes begin absorbing more pressure to relieve the injured part and enable us to walk without losing our balance. Every organism and every adjacent area makes a contribution, either by pulling additional weight or contributing nutrients, until the injured body part is healed.

Examining the human body suggests important parallels for needed succession planning strategies.

◆ **We must individually value succession.** Just as the body begins reproducing itself internally before it's mature enough to reproduce externally, we must place a high value on succession planning. We cannot expect to have an organization that values succession and develops others if the senior leadership does not think and act accordingly. If the founder, the CEO or the senior pastor hasn't developed a transition plan and isn't mentoring, we cannot expect the rest of the organization's leaders to be receptive to these ideas.

◆ **Reproduction should become an innate characteristic.** Our bodies are constantly reproducing new cells without conscious thought or effort. In the same way, when we act consistently with the value that we place on succession planning, our organization develops a culture of succession. We can start this simply by delegating certain duties to other individuals. If we find that someone else can do a job as well or better than we can, it should become their responsibility. When they're able to discharge that duty, it allows us to function on new levels and become a greater asset to the organization.

◆ **Our organizations must be prepared to function in our absence.** Many leaders react negatively—primarily out of insecurity—to the thought of developing someone else to succeed them. That thinking is akin to believing that a broken toe will shut down the entire body. We must value our organizations enough to develop other leaders into successors. Whenever we develop another person to succeed us, or it happens elsewhere in the hierarchy, it adds value to the organization and ensures its future success. Eventually, all of the leaders in the ministry or the business will follow that example. This can begin in small ways. For example, the information systems manager can create documents that tell others how to correct system problems. By doing this, and training an assistant, it ensures that the smooth operation of the enterprise isn't dependent on any one person. In their absence, everything will still flow seamlessly.

> **Succession must be a progressive work that adheres to the Inward–Outward–Upward–Onward sequence.**

Developing an effective succession plan and creating a dynamic, reproductive leadership culture doesn't happen overnight. There are generally four progressive steps to this process.

1. **Inward**—God begins to internally birth the idea or a vision within you. In this stage, you begin considering the benefits to yourself and your organization, asking questions, seeking information, and weighing the many personal and organizational issues and implications.

2. **Outward**—At some point, you become comfortable enough to begin discussions with your management team, your board, your family, and other important stakeholders.

3. **Upward**—Nothing that we do personally or collectively is ready to proceed until we lift it up to God. As we give our thoughts and plans to Him, we're effectively saying, "God, separate the wheat from the chaff. Do whatever you have to do to refine this." It may not be necessary or worthwhile for

us to reproduce everything in our tradition; some things should be blown away by the winds of time. Other things can be pruned and refined to cause them to yield new life.

4. Onward—Once the plans have been created, refined and blessed, they are ready to yield dividends to future generations.

Succession must be a progressive work that adheres to the Inward–Outward–Upward–Onward sequence. If our plans go outward without sufficient internal development, they risk sounding hollow. And plans that are implemented too early are destined for failure because they neglect vital issues and concerns. Too many times, succession plans fall flat because we have not done the critical spadework and preparation. Only after we mull over our thoughts inwardly, bring them outward, and lift everything up to God are we ready to go onward.

Encouragement for the Journey

The Old Testament prophets were dynamic visionaries. The prophet Elisha gained distinction by being mentored by the legendary Elijah. As Elijah's successor and protégé, Elisha was blessed with a double portion of Elijah's spirit. He was considered twice as effective as his famous mentor—with twice his skills, talents and rich capabilities.

Unfortunately, Elisha lacked a trusted successor to take his place. His servant and understudy, Gehazi, was a likely prospect until he seized Elisha's authority and disqualified himself. When Elisha died, there was no mention of Gehazi or of any successor.

Elisha literally took his anointing to the grave. When a dead body was thrown into the same grave and touched Elisha's bones, the dead man was revived[10]. The anointing, the God-imparted gifts and wisdom that Elisha possessed were designed for earth. There was no need for these gifts in heaven; the ability to destroy oppressive yokes and lift heavy burdens was designed for use upon the earth.

If we don't find—or don't search for—someone we can invest in, we'll take our abilities to the grave like Elisha. There are far too many cemeteries that are loaded with skill and with anointed wisdom because insecure leaders did not want to give up their power. Because they didn't know how to find—or didn't care to find—younger leaders they could empower with their gifts, future generations were robbed of a blessing.

> **Too many cemeteries are loaded with skill and with anointed wisdom because insecure leaders did not want to give up their power.**

It's a great tragedy for a leader to be without a successor. If we are unwilling to pass the baton, to accept that we must decrease and they must increase, the gifts and talents we have that were designed to be wonders in the earth will never find their release in the future. We must give our successors roots and foundations, providing them with wings to fly higher than we have, and applauding them along the way.

Many of us must deal with the personal insecurity that hinders us. We must begin searching for a connection, for protégés who can serve honestly and without ulterior motives. We have a responsibility to seek them out.

The task of finding a protégé to succeed us may be easier than many of us might think. They are also looking for us. There are younger leaders in your organization, in your church, and in your business who are looking, who are ready, and who need someone to recognize and develop their potential.

Like the nursing mother and her child, we are searching for each other. When a mother hears her baby's cry, her milk begins to flow, spurring her to action. When we nourish our successors, it becomes an incredible blessing—both for us and for future generations.

We do not need to live in default any longer. We don't need to create chaos in our organizations by leaving their leadership futures in question. We can begin living by design. We can ensure that our vision, our passion, our wisdom and our experience transcend the current generation.

Assessing the
Avoidance Factors

Most of us are no strangers to planning.

We envision and manage highly successful organizations. We design and launch complex products and services to meet anticipated customer needs. We prepare the sermons and the presentations that communicate with our members, our associates, our employees, and our boards. We ensure that our organizations acquire the funding and the resources required to achieve defined objectives.

In that context, isn't it perplexing that so many of us continue pushing our succession plans to the backburner? We readily acknowledge the need for planning these leadership transitions. We read articles and books or attend workshop sessions on the topic. Some of us even lie awake at night considering and evaluating the many factors. In the end, however, we're not moving toward the finish line, but the finish line continues racing toward us.

Why do we avoid developing and implementing these plans? There are no simple answers. In our discussions with many organizational leaders, we've witnessed a number of inter-related factors.

Some are easy to detect; others hide deep inside of us, evading our own conscious discernment.

Our inaction is caused by complex factors. Let's face it: If faced with a simple issue, most of us are resourceful enough to execute the necessary decisions to quickly resolve it. When we're facing succession planning, however, we're not dealing with a simple case of supply and demand. We're dealing with an intricate web of motivations, feelings, basic needs and organizational situations. Tugging on one end of this tangled fishing line invariably produces reactions and results elsewhere.

Despite the many intricacies, we've grouped the major factors affecting succession planning into four broad categories. The issues that we'll be examining have their roots primarily in our:

- Brains
- Hearts
- Contexts
- Resources

Brain Matters

Many years before I (Dr. Bronner) founded my current church—the Word of Faith Family Worship Cathedral in Austell, GA—I launched an innovative ministry in my public high school that affected the entire 2,000-member student body on a weekly basis. As a teenager, I successfully proclaimed the Gospel and built a healthy student fellowship over a three-year period.

When I graduated, this ministry essentially died. Upon learning of this, I remember being grieved and a little angry with God.

It was my first opportunity to learn important lessons about succession planning.

Like many founders, I had given little conscious thought to what would happen when I left. I *assumed* that things would just work themselves out or that God would help the next person, just as He helped me. God made it clear why this high-school ministry died, telling me, "It died because you didn't teach someone what I taught you."

I mistakenly thought that whatever was true for me would be true for the next person to assume leadership of the school fellowship. Since I had nothing to read to help me organize the ministry, it didn't occur to me that anyone else would need written guidance. Since I was able to rely on God, I thought **All change involves loss.** that God would also pass along whatever was necessary to the next ministry leader. I never thought that God was relying on me to pass the baton.

Upon realizing that I had a responsibility to pass along what I had learned, I created a small manual to help other high schoolers to establish similar ministries. I wished that I had taken the opportunity to do more when I still had the chance.

For example, I could have brought in a younger student and developed that person to plan and run the meetings. I would have taught this successor how to structure each meeting for variety, as well as how to ensure that they respected everyone's time by starting and ending promptly.

Most importantly, I would have taught the younger leader how to prepare their own successor. By having a younger leader walk alongside me, I could have passed along the values that captured the spirit and mission of the ministry, which enabled the creation of a godly counter-culture.

When thinking about succession, many leaders make the same errors that I made:

- We make assumptions about the abilities and the situations of those who may come after us, thinking that they'll be similar to ours.
- We think that situations will take care of themselves.
- We don't consider how much we have to pass along.
- We don't see that we have a responsibility to provide the blessing of our experience to someone else.

In each of these cases, *it's our wrong thinking that justifies our inaction.*

Those of us who are *change resistant* find further support and justification for inaction. Even if we comprehend the need for action,

> **Tomorrow's leaders must be ready to lead differently than yesterday's leaders. They must appreciate the past without trying to recreate it.**

the discomfort inherent in change keeps us from moving forward. We resist change because all change involves loss.

This life is constantly in flux. We can no more stop the cycle of change than we can stem the ocean tides. Change is constant; none of us can afford to deny it. But we do have to get our thinking in synch with the facts.

This resistance to change could be rooted in unclear thinking about the future. When Moses was leading Israel, for example, they were nomads. They didn't plant crops; they gathered the manna and quail that were provided for them. When Joshua followed Moses into leadership, his generation had to become more agricultural as they settled the land. They also had to be more warrior-like because they had to fight to take this land. The times and the cultures of these two leaders were very different.

We cannot assume that what-ever is true today will be true tomor-row. Each generation has to be able to connect to the existing culture and

> **Develop a healthier self-image, one that can separate our net worth from our self-worth.**

present the gospel appropriately for that time. That means that tomorrow's leaders must be ready to lead differently than yester-day's leaders. Tomorrow's leaders cannot rely upon yesterday's prac-tices and processes; they must forge new paths in new directions and anticipate future possibilities. They should study the past, but not be content to rest on their successes. They must appreciate the past without trying to recreate it.

Heart Conditions

Our western culture encourages us to spend many years prepar-ing for our chosen careers. Once we've gotten the necessary degrees and qualifications, we invest many more years gaining experience, applying ourselves, setting and reaching goals, and continuing the achievement cycle. It's no surprise that we might be unsettled by the notion of being without this daily routine, of no longer doing work that we've found fulfilling.

Surveys on our feelings about retirement are quite telling. When asked about their retirement goals by the National Federation of Independent Businesses, nearly 70 percent of small-business owners said they don't *ever* plan to retire. If they do, they'll do so only when they're well past the traditional retirement age.[11]

Commenting on this study, one financial planner concluded that it was no surprise, adding that he wished he had the psychological background to help his clients deal with the many emotional issues standing between them and retirement.

"Financial planning is the easy piece," he said. "Most owners have to be convinced there is life after retirement."[12]

Business people aren't the only ones who feel threatened by retirement. It's equally evident in pastors, in leaders of non-profits, and in other organizations. Men are particularly prone to confuse who they are with what they do. Many of us may need to develop a healthier self-image, one that can separate our net worth from our self-worth.

> The biggest reason for avoiding succession planning may be that it forces us to face our own mortality.

We need to stop and answer some important questions.

- Are we resisting succession planning because it forces us to analyze and evaluate ourselves, to pause and take a deep look inside?
- Are we avoiding moving forward because this analysis reveals character flaws—our own vices, our bad habits, our mediocrity, and our sin?
- Are we marking time until we can correct these flaws, so that this seed doesn't multiply in the next generation of leadership?

Perhaps the biggest reason for avoiding succession planning may be that it forces us to face our own mortality. "Too many business owners are married to the business," said a consultant who conducts strategic planning seminars for the Council of Smaller Enterprises. "As a result, they equate retirement with death."[13]

No one is immune to fears about death, not even those of us who are sought out by others for advice on matters of faith. Baby Boomers have shown themselves to be particularly uncomfortable with aging—spending millions on anti-wrinkle creams, cosmetic surgery, hair dye and other products that promise to make us look younger. We worry about becoming useless, dependent on others, or ending up as invalids. Since succession planning is a big step toward a potentially undesirable direction, it's understandable that we delay it as long as possible.

In his book *Aging is an Attitude,* author Cecil Murphey relates a story about a friend who wanted to introduce him to a business associate. During this conversation, his friend referred to him as "an older man." Murphey—who was 51 at the time—didn't hear the rest of what his friend said. All he could think about was that he had just been called "old." Driving home, he

> **I view retirement as a time for doing what I want to do, not what I have to do.**

remembered a comment by Oliver Wendell Holmes: "A person is always startled when he hears himself seriously called an old man for the first time."

Like Murphey, many of us need to examine our feelings about our own aging. We may have to begin focusing on the benefits and the advantages of this stage of life. Rather than living in denial, we have to get a grasp on what Murphey calls "positive aging."

"I focus on aging as a positive factor in my life," he writes. "If God planned for us to get older, why should I argue and call this phase of life negative? Is it possible, I asked myself, that God intended the last years to be the best? Instead of sinking into oblivion, could the divine plan encourage us to sing the hymns of triumph all the way to the grave? Can it be that God wants us to enjoy our final part of the journey as much as we did the first two parts? Perhaps enjoy it even more?"[14]

Along with a healthy view of aging, many of us need a vision and a purpose for the latter years of our lives. Unless we're drawn to desirable retirement goals, we'll likely avoid any notion of succession planning. We need a larger vision of the options that are available to us. Too many of us think in limited terms because we don't see anything else that we can do. That causes us to hang onto the only job security, to the only purpose we know.

I (Dr. Chand) view retirement as a time for doing what I want to do, not what I have to do. It doesn't mean that I will stop working, go into seclusion or hang up the gloves. Like most leaders, I plan on including some work in my retirement. I see it as a time for expanding my options.

Connect with your dreams. Think about what you would love to do during your retirement years. Maybe you've always wanted to teach or write. If you're a pastor, you could be available to other churches, using your expertise to help a larger flock. Business owners might want to serve in a non-profit organization, bringing them a particularly needed skill. Start liberating yourself by thinking about where you could be. That might be enough motivation to begin succession planning, to equip others to function in your absence.

Context Complexities

Neglect of succession planning can be attributed to our busyness, to the complexities of the marketplace, and the overall pace of life. The rapid changes in markets and mindsets have kept us so preoccupied with success—or with survival—that we have little time to devote to succession.

Tim Elmore, the president of Growing Leaders, says that market growth in the 20th century drove business schools to emphasize management over leadership due to the increased need to manage our organizations, our businesses, and our markets. This emphasis on man-

> **Success without a successor is failure.**

agement led to a rise in bureaucracy and in institutionalized cultures, which discouraged employees from learning to lead.[15]

"Change happened so fast during the 20th century that established leaders often neglected to address the need to prepare future leaders," he writes. "Leaders were so consumed with keeping up with the pace of business that they couldn't focus on the need to mentor next-generation leaders. It was all they could do to survive the present day."

Elmore refers to the vacuum created in leadership ranks and the resulting lack of succession planning as "The Joshua Problem." The Old Testament tells the story of Moses bringing God's people to the Jordan River, to the edge of the Promised Land. At that point, Moses handed the reigns of leadership to his apprentice, Joshua. Because Joshua didn't prepare a successor, however, Israel was thrown into chaos when he died. Judges 21:25 tersely summarized the resulting era by saying, "And there was no king in Israel in those days, and everyone did what was right in his own eyes."

"What folks fail to realize is that Moses' greatest achievement might have been the years he invested mentoring young Joshua," writes Elmore. "Somehow, he knew what Dr. Carl Henry has summarized so well: Success without a successor is failure."[16]

Resource Constraints

According to one consultant who has advised business own-ers for more than 20 years, too many business owners stay too long, lag industry trends, and don't create sufficient value in their busi-nesses. Because they live for the moment rather than plan for the future, many of them are financially unable to retire.[17]

Financial security plagues leaders in a variety of organizations. When I (Dr. Chand) talk with pastors and organizational leaders about succession planning, I've learned not to assume that they have their financial houses in order. Some churches and organizations may not even provide retirement funds or pensions.

> "It's better to train a hundred men than to do the work of a hundred men," wrote D.L Moody. "But it is harder."

While those in this position may want to pursue other options, we may avoid succession planning simply because we need the job and the associated financial security. Financial necessities will force us to continue working until our health fails, we become incompe-tent, or we die. While understandable, these organizational envi-ronments may not be the best breeding grounds for continued excellence, profitability or longevity.

Those who may be ready to implement succession plans, typically find ourselves facing another problem. Simply put, we don't have many paradigms to follow or to study. We may not have access to mentors or sources with the specific experience that we need. Without an appropriate model, we may be unwilling or unable to devote much time to researching our options.

Proposing a Path Forward

We are clearly in need of a paradigm shift in our thinking and practice about leadership transitions and succession planning. In the remainder of this book, we hope to provide some workable ideas and solutions.

- Chapter 3—Models of Succession Planning—dissects both successful and unsuccessful models of succession in businesses, churches and other organizations.
- Chapter 4—Selecting and Developing Successors—examines methods for finding and growing a protégé.
- Chapter 5—Making a Graceful Exit—provides guidance in developing a purpose beyond our current position, which can benefit our organizations, our successors, and us.
- Chapter 6—Considerations for Successors—offers suggestions to help our protégés to avoid common problems and maximize their opportunities.

"It's better to train a hundred men than to do the work of a hundred men," wrote D.L Moody. "But it is harder." Succession planning is also complex, difficult work. We're not suggesting that there is a simple solution that will work in all organizations. In fact, just the opposite is true. The best succession plans and the most appropriate transitions are custom designed. Still, there are many valid principles and best practices that are worth discussing, following, modifying and sharing.

While the issues may be difficult, there is a promising goal calling us onward: The succession plans that we create for our organizations may well become blessings for generations to come.

Models for
Succession Planning

What separates successful and unsuccessful succession plans? The jury is still out on this question. However, as the executive ranks continue aging, the turnover rate will change that, providing models for us to follow, as well as revealing models for us to avoid.

> We're navigating uncharted territory without a good map— only a compass.

For now, it seems that we're navigating uncharted territory without a good map—only a compass. "There's almost no scientific research on succession that shows what works and what doesn't," says Joe Astrachan, PhD, director of the Cox Family Enterprise Center at Kennesaw (Ga.) State University.[18]

Those of us currently considering our own succession may not have the luxury of waiting for another generation to provide map points, explain principles and benchmark their best practices. We'll have to examine whatever evidence we can find, whether it's from an orderly transition of power or a headline-making failure.

While this chapter is organized into sections that describe succession in family businesses, churches, non-profits and corporations, the principles in each section are applicable in any organization. The cases and examples in each section are just one way of answering some important questions:

- What best *practices* can we follow?
- What *actions* should be avoided?
- What *principles* should be understood?

Family Business Transitions

My father—Nathaniel Bronner—and my uncle Arthur started Bronner Brothers in 1947. Today, my brothers run that same company, with my brother Bernard at the helm. After the successful transfer of the company from my father in 1993, we began diversifying the family business to expand it beyond its primary focus on hair-care products. The company now includes other successful endeavors, including a magazine and a health products business. While I'm not actively involved in the day-to-day operation of the company, I do sit on the board of directors.

It was a conversation with Dr. Benjamin Elijah Mays—who was Martin Luther King's mentor—that got Dad considering succession planning. Dr. Mays had seen businesses in the Atlanta area that didn't survive past the founder's generation because no thought was given to these transitions. Often, when the founder's children inherited the company, it slowly crumbled. This prompted Dr. Mays to ask my dad, "Bronner, what are you doing to ensure that when you die, your business does not die with you?"

At the time, Dad was only in his late forties. It was probably hard for him to get a grasp on his own mortality at that age. A few years later, however, he had a "wake-up call" in the form of a heart attack. Remembering the poignant question from Dr. Mays, he began considering his own succession and preparing his sons. He also began changing his diet and exercise habits. The doctors told him that if he abandoned his business, modified his diet and his lifestyle that he might live another two years. Dad lived another 30 years. I'm sure that Dr. Mays' question continued reverberating in his mind during that time.

We recommend starting the process as early as possible. Churches and companies should begin thinking about succession when they pass the volatile start-up years. For family businesses, we suggest that even before children are born that the owners have discussions about how ownership and leadership might be transferred. We also stress the importance of giving children an early sense of responsibility.

> **"When you live in the shadow of a big tree, you have to run twice as fast to get into the sunlight."**

My father was an advocate of starting early, so my brothers and I were exposed to work early in our lives. He never gave us an allowance. He exposed us to the feel and the flavor of business while we were young, giving us an opportunity to earn money in the process. We worked as stock boys in the warehouse, as well as selling money orders and running the register in our drug store.

My first exposure to the business world came at the age of five. My dad took me around the neighborhood and we knocked on doors together, asking neighbors if they would allow me to deliver *The Atlanta Daily World* to them. I held that job for fifteen years.

My older brothers also delivered newspapers. We all learned to take care of our customers, keep track of who owed us money, and manage the profit.

Paper routes and working in Dad's company communicated many valuable lessons early in life. Working taught me that money doesn't grow on trees. Through working, I also realized that the world doesn't owe me anything and grasped the importance of going out and creating opportunities. Because Dad introduced all of my brothers to the value of work, we never felt privileged. Instead, we inherited a valuable work ethic and a tradition from our father.

When I was twelve, I started helping with the company payroll. We had no computers then, so my strong math skills came in handy. It also helped that my mother was an accountant. I calculated the hours each person worked, multiplying it by an hourly rate to determine a gross salary. I took out the taxes and arrived at net pay, manually writing all the payroll checks by hand. Over the years, I walked through the process of getting all of that computerized.

> **Most of us planning leadership transitions aren't thinking about how differently the world will be for those coming after us.**

It didn't always seem like work; there was a certain amount of fun in being exposed to different areas of the business. Often, my dad just threw us into something new. Since my uncles had sales routes in Georgia, Alabama and South Carolina, he introduced us to sales by having us travel with them. During the latter part of my high school years and during college, I earned my money by working in the manufacturing plants as a batch compound formulator. I mixed the chemicals and went through the process of making them in huge vats. When that was done, the line workers used that mixture in the product packaging.

There was another benefit to our working in Dad's company, aside from the valuable work experience we gained. In some companies, when family members begin heading up or working in the business, resentment is evident in other workers. They question their qualifications for their positions, making claims of nepotism. Even when my brothers rose into management, we never experienced that. One reason was because our business was relatively small at the time. More importantly, by having us rise through the ranks like everyone else and work in every position, we didn't seem like outsiders who were being given authority that we hadn't earned. We had legitimacy, we had earned our credentials and our competency was not questioned.

Many family businesses follow similar paths to enable family members to prove themselves. Before Paul Jacobs succeeded his father Irwin, the founder of the wireless technology firm Qualcomm, he put in a number of years in the firm's engineering division. It wasn't the patents he created that eventually earned him the CEO slot; it was a successful stint at running a start-up division that manufactured wireless phones. Despite his lack of experience in operations, the division was so successful that it was sold to a Japanese company for an undisclosed amount. Two years later, when the board of directors began looking for a successor for his 68-year old father, he was ready.

The Estee Lauder cosmetics firm is now in its third-generation of family management. Three months after his grandmother died, William Lauder took over as CEO, filling the position previously held by his father. The position wasn't handed to him easily. He reports being regularly questioned about business matters at family dinners, and also recalls spending one college spring break in Tokyo, where he accompanied his father on visits to retail stores. His father even required him to get experience somewhere else, prompting William to work for Macy's for a number of years.

Establishing his own leadership credibility wasn't easy, he says. In one *Fortune* magazine interview, he said, "I have to work twice as hard for half the credit primarily because of who I am and why I am here." The same article recalls that William reportedly told *The New York Times* "When you live in the shadow of a big tree, you have to run twice as fast to get into the sunlight."[19]

Whatever credibility family members build among employees and stakeholders can be quickly destroyed by sibling rivalry and squabbling. Dad knew this instinctively. Here, he did more than teach us this lesson; his entire generation modeled this critical quality for us. After they founded the business, Dad and my uncle brought their sister into the company, a move that wasn't prompted by feelings of obligation. We witnessed each of them working in positions that matched their unique gifts, so much so that none clamored for the other's position.

My dad was a family man before he was a businessman. He emphasized that we were a team, whether we were working in the yard or cleaning out the basement. Family and teamwork were always preeminent. As a result, there were no conflicts about who would eventually succeed him. There were no questions about it either. At an early age, my oldest brother, Nathaniel, somehow knew that he wasn't suited to the task. When Bernard was born, a five-year old Nathaniel pointed at him and said, "There's the president." His youthful insight proved incredibly accurate. Today, Nathaniel remains a successful chemist within our company. As a scientist, his competencies are not those needed in an effective CEO. Bernard, on the other hand, is gregarious, outgoing and has the other important and necessary business qualifications. There was never any question about who possessed the right skills for this job; we all knew this early in the ballgame.

Normally, there's a fair amount of bickering in family-owned entities. Our family business is a rare exception to the rule. The estate-planning attorneys we use have marveled at our harmony, telling us that they've never worked with such a cohesive group. They even asked to spend time with us socially so they could observe us outside the work environment. The difference for us is the example set by my dad, a strong visionary leader. Because the next generation didn't directly experience his leadership and direction, I wonder if they'll have this same conflict-free environment.

Family-owned companies are a critical part of our free-enterprise system. Of the estimated 21 million small businesses in the US, 90 percent are family owned. However, only 30 percent succeed into a second generation and only 15 percent make it to the third generation.[20] A mere 20 percent of family businesses last more than 60 years.[21]

> **Those of us considering successors should be ready to celebrate their achievements whenever we can.**

These facts should motivate family businesses to take steps to ensure that their disagreements don't affect the bottom line. Regular family board meetings with open discussions should be an on-going occurrence. The cousins running Estee Lauder schedule routine meetings to discuss operations, even bringing in a moderator when necessary. The value they place on the family legacy led them to ensure that they were always walking in agreement. "We are not a family business," their written manifesto states, "We are a family in business." Jane Lauder emphasized the value of their legacy to

Fortune magazine, "My grandparents did such an incredible job building this company and gave us so many advantages, that you want to be able to keep it going."[22]

The value of Bronner Brothers isn't in the shares we own or in the cash endowments that we can spend. It's in the character, the competencies and the contributions that my dad, my uncle and aunt made. If we value that inheritance and always retain that perspective, the rest of the legacy tends to take care of itself.

Today, we're in the process of preparing the next generation. We have a field of 30 potential successors standing in the wings and are passing along the same lessons that my father gave to us, using many of the same methods. Like us, the children started working in the business while they were young, with a goal of enabling them to be familiar with the operations by the time they reach college age. While the next CEO hasn't yet emerged, we're hopeful about the results. "I believe we'll be around for at least the next 100 years," my brothers told one reporter. "Same principles, same result."[23]

Succession for Churches and Non-Profits

In addition to providing guidance on succession planning to hundreds of companies, churches and organizations, I (Dr. Chand) personally have experienced many transitions in my career, and I will highlight two of the more significant ones here.

The first occurred when I left my pastorate at a church in Michigan. Here, I planned the transition together with the board and was involved in bringing on my replacement. Some years later, I successfully transitioned my role as president of Beulah Heights University to Dr. Benson Karanja, which is described in my book

Who Moved Your Ladder. Each of these situations provided me with many valuable insights that I continue to build upon.

While pastoring in Michigan, I was presented with the opportunity to take the position at Beulah Heights University, which was then Beulah Heights Bible College in Atlanta, Georgia. Before I made my decision, I sought the wisdom of the church board and included them in my decision-making process. For a number of weeks, I met with the elders and had many healthy conversations as we thought through all of the associated questions. All of them clearly wanted me to stay, but they graciously saw the big picture and encouraged me to move ahead.

Once the decision was made in December, I announced my resignation by sending a letter to the church in January. On one hand, I did what everyone writing about succession planning says to do: set a timeframe and stick to it. My mistake was making the resignation effective in June; the six months between the announcement and my departure was too long. There were too many opportunities for me to make decisions and start programs that someone else would have to live with. I wasn't aware of this at the time; I didn't even realize it until I got feedback during the exit interviews that I conducted with my leaders.

It's also a mistake for any leader to give a resignation and say that he or she is willing to stay until the organization finds a replacement. That situation isn't good for the leader or for the organization. Unless the organization feels some sense of urgency to find a replacement, the leader will have to linger. Since that person is likely feeling more of a pull toward the new venture, they may not be giving their best. If necessary, there can be some mutual agreement about achieving certain goals or benchmarks prior to the departure.

For me, achieving accreditation for the college and preparing a successor were important, as were meeting certain financial benchmarks and filling spots for two department chairpersons. Once those goals were achieved, I knew that it was time to move on.

In both situations, I was involved in naming my successor. For the new pastor, we selected a gentleman who had been part of the same country church many years earlier. Because he knew the people and the environment, it seemed like a good fit, especially since he was eager about coming back. What we didn't realize was that the new pastor and others in the congregation thought that they were going to pick up where they left off some 20 years earlier, not realizing how the church had grown and changed in the meantime. Someone should have thought more about the changes that occurred and prepared this new pastor. He was coming back to a very different place.

Most of us planning leadership transitions aren't thinking about how differently the world will be for those coming after us. Like the pastor that succeeded me, or the congregation he worked with, we think things will be the same. But the pace of change is only accelerating, which means our leaders and our organizations need to be better prepared. There are more churches and organizations being founded than ever before. Even the churches being planted now have a more entrepreneurial edge, with multi-site and multi-location groups springing up all over. It's truly a different world.

> **Certain qualities make entrepreneurial founders a different breed from those who follow them. In contrast, their successors lack one critical attribute: courage.**

At Beulah Heights, I also had the opportunity to select my successor and to involve the board, but I handled this situation quite differently. I realized initially that a bigger jet needed a longer runway. In a small organization, two to three months is more than adequate for a good transition. Since the university had a more significant impact and more stakeholders, we needed a longer transition.

I had been quietly planning the transition for three years before I gave my resignation. During this time, in addition to meeting certain goals and benchmarks, I had been busily preparing my successor. I began positioning Dr. Karanja by having him replace me on certain committees, stand in for me at various

> **Matching a strategic need to a leader's experience is what characterized success.**

ous functions and also introduced him to key people. Not even Dr. Karanja knew that he was being mentored as my replacement.

As I started thinking about vocalizing my planned departure, I sought out a wider perspective in the counsel that I received. When I left the church, I only sought out the collective input of the elders on that particular church board. At the college, I spoke individually to 13 different leaders who had gone through major transitions. Having that diverse input enabled me to see many additional aspects of the same situation. It made a difference in the outcome.

When it was time for me to go, this time I didn't linger. I announced my resignation in mid-October and my final day as president was the end of December. I told Dr. Karanja that he could call me for advice during his first year as president. After that, he needed to be fully in charge. I purposely didn't even set foot on the campus for nearly eight months after resigning. The transition has been wonderful to watch. The school expanded from college to university status, initiated a graduate program, and many other new endeavors. I've been happy to see it rising higher.

We should not neglect the importance of celebrating both our

organization's past and its future. Every year, I formally communicate with Dr. Karanja just to recount all of his successes and remind
him of my on-going support. Sadly, this didn't happen when I visited
my former pastorate in Michigan one holiday. Because my family
lived in the area, we attended that church for a Christmas service.
As a courtesy, I had called my successor to advise him that I would
be visiting. Many people greeted us warmly and even asked if I would
be speaking. There was not a single acknowledgement of our presence from the pulpit on that Sunday morning.

Those of us considering successors should be ready to celebrate their achievements whenever we can; those moving into these
positions should never forget the past or the contributions of those
who preceded them. While Solomon may have built the legendary
temple in Israel, for example, he was indebted to the foundation
laid by his father David. Leaders, stakeholders, board members and
church members all need to see the unbroken chain that links the
past and the future because it provides hope. It's what motivates
everyone to move forward into an uncertain future and energizes
our daily activities.

Corporate Transitions

Bigger isn't necessarily better. Whether they're trying to replace
a visionary founder or a CEO, corporations face their fair share of
challenges. In addition to dealing with board-related issues, they
have to satisfy shareholder expectations and ensure that stock prices
and annual revenues aren't negatively affected.

Succeeding a company's founder is a thankless job. To borrow
one show-business phrase, stepping into any visionary founder's

shoes is simply "a tough act to follow." There are countless reports of problems.

The tension between founders and successors was visible at one recent high-level gathering. Three pairs of founder and successors—from Microsoft, Yahoo and Facebook—made appearances at a conference hosted by *The Wall Street Journal*, prompting a related article to remark that, "While all the speakers did their best to make nice, it didn't take a Geiger counter to sense that offstage, each management team might have a few issues to work out."[24]

> **"When the strategic need matched the strategic experience of the hired GE executive, companies saw annualized abnormal returns of 14.1 percent while mismatched pairings saw returns of −39.8 percent."**

Some tension between founders and successors can be the result of conflicting ambitions. Founders tend to have a high regard for their abilities simply because they've started and run a successful organization. It can be difficult for them to tolerate any leader who doesn't appear to be on the same level. While problems typically occur in companies with 60- or 70-year old founders who are reluctant to leave, having a strong-willed founder who hasn't reached 40 is a recipe for even greater tension.

Some founders never learn how to gracefully make room for their successors, giving management schools decades of examples to study and dissect. "These are timeless issues," one professor from Northwestern University's Kellogg School of Management told *The Wall Street Journal*. In some cases, it takes a second or third start-up for a founder to realize the importance of passing the baton.[25]

Even after a founder leaves, the story might not be over. In some versions of this familiar story, a founder comes out of retirement when his company begins failing under the leadership of its new CEO. This was the case when Michael Dell returned to the computer company bearing his name to replace CEO Kevin Rollins and when Nike founder Phil Knight returned to oust Bill Perez.

What's the source of this problem? A recent *Forbes* article provided some insight by describing how certain qualities make entrepreneurial founders a different breed from those who follow them. The article reports that the biggest difference appears to be how founders rebound from failure. "True entrepreneurs like Michael Dell, Charles Schwab and Steve Jobs have hit the wall of disappointment and know how to reinvent themselves and discover heroic new missions for their enterprise."[26]

In contrast, their successors lack one critical attribute: courage. "Too often, those who follow an entrepreneur—like Nardelli at Home Depot—tend to focus on internal systems or ritualize past practices, without the visionary risk-taking courage of those who've experienced or learned from prior setbacks."[27]

Given the difficulties in replacing a founder, how does a company avoid making mistakes? According to *Harvard Business Review*, the secret might be in ensuring a match between the candidate's skills and the company's strategic needs. Researchers at GE categorized the skills of 20 executives, following their transitions to determine how they fared when matched with appropriate strategic challenges. The researchers characterized leaders by three skill types:

> **"The world's best speedboat captain isn't able to pilot an oil tanker."**

- A talent for cost cutting and being price competitive (cost controllers)
- The ability to sustain growth (growers)

- Skills for surviving in highly cyclical businesses (cycle managers).

The best predictor of approaching problems was a mismatch between a leader and a company's strategic challenge. "Not all managers are equally suited to all business situations," they reported. "When the telecommunications industry was deregulated and challenged by new entrants, for instance, few former Bell Systems managers were able to successfully transition to the fast-moving, entrepreneurial, growth-oriented environment, despite being seasoned veterans of what was considered one of America's best-managed companies."[28]

> **Rather than looking for someone with the same DNA, you have to determine what direction the organization will be taking in the long-term and look for someone who can chart the course.**

Matching a strategic need to a leader's experience is what characterized success, they determined. Examples cited included growth driver Steve Bennet, who launched new businesses and increased profits substantially at the software company Intuit. Carlos Ghosn used his skill as a cost cutter to successfully lead turnarounds for Nissan, Michelin and Goodrich-Uniroyal.

The right combination of skill and strategic challenge could produce heady revenues, just as the wrong ones yielded dismal failures. "When the strategic need matched the strategic experience of the hired GE executive, companies saw annualized abnormal returns of 14.1 percent while mismatched pairings saw returns of −39.8 percent."[29]

Other examples echo this recommendation. After Wily Technology's board-initiated a search for a new CEO to help the company chart a new course, founder Lew Cirine agreed to take a position as chief-technology officer. Realizing that his gifts no longer matched the company's needs, Cirine said, "the world's best speedboat captain isn't able to pilot an oil tanker."[30]

While founders possess admirable entrepreneurial skills, not many appear equally well suited to the task of successfully managing an enterprise. "People like Bill Gates and Larry Ellison, who are able to lead their companies for quite a while, get all the attention because they are rare, not because they are typical," says one Harvard Business School report. "Not many company founders go on to become successful CEOs."[31]

> "Successors typically fall into two categories—those representing continuity and those representing change."

Once a company is launched, business challenges can change dramatically, causing a founder to take command of somewhat less satisfying duties, such as leading a sales organization or managing growing financial complexities. In privately held companies, a founder without the right team might find the company headed toward the rocks. In public companies, where control is traded in return for capitalization, it's not unusual for the board to replace a founder to make way for a professional CEO.

Consciously or unconsciously searching for a mirror image of the departing CEO or founder can further complicate the search for a successor. Looking for someone like the person being replaced limits your direction, only giving you more of what you already had. Rather than looking for someone with the same DNA, you have to determine what direction the organization will be taking in the long-term and look for someone who can chart the course.

Many organizations wrestle with the traditional question of whether they should go with an internal candidate or an external one. Companies listed in the S&P 500 tend to hire CEOs from the outside in one-third of the cases. Typically, taking a search outside the company is regarded as a vote of "no confidence" in the internal candidates. It may also indicate that the company requires a specific skill set to solve particular problems. Troubles increase the tendency to look for external candidates to 40 percent.[32]

Corporate America has many examples of CEOs stepping aside to be replaced by familiar insiders. When Bill Gates stepped down as CEO in 2000 to run his foundation, he handed the baton to company President Steve Ballmer. Before this transition, these two leaders had known each other for more than 25 years. Allstate selected the company's president to replace the outgoing CEO, citing their ten-year working relationship and a "shared passion for the industry." Target also selected its number-two man to replace CEO Robert Ulrich.

> **Most bylaws and similar governing documents are written for yesterday, not for tomorrow.**

A *Fortune* article aptly summed up the deciding criteria. "Successors typically fall into two categories—those representing continuity, like Steve Ballmer at Microsoft, and those representing change, like Jack Welch."[33]

Succession-Planning Principles

The research on successful and troubled succession plans offers a wealth of ideas to pass along, as well as counsel on paths to avoid. While some of this information may seem obvious, it's never a bad idea to ensure that you're building on a good foundation.

◆ **Have an emergency plan.** In addition to preparing a succession plan for your retirement or other transitions, give some thought to what should transpire if you were to die suddenly or become incapacitated. Create a shortlist with details about who needs to be contacted and what discussions should occur. In most cases, the list either specifies a successor or instructs the board to name a replacement. Most executives have a shortlist that details what happens in these cases and informs an assistant or the board of its location.

◆ **Consider bylaws.** Most bylaws and similar governing documents are written for yesterday, not for tomorrow. Since succession is about creating an organization's future, this can be problematic. Most bylaws contain rules that have their own history. For example, if the church bylaws say that any elder candidate must be a member for a minimum of three years, it's likely because someone messed up early in their tenure. The board said, "Never again," and made a rule to enforce it. Make sure that bylaws are inspected and updated periodically so they aren't unnecessarily restrictive. Ensure they provide a foundation for designing a bright future rather than just defending against past mistakes.

◆ **Get help from outside consultants.** Getting a consultant who can survey the land and help you to work through the relevant issues is important. Ideally, this should be someone with the necessary objectivity, experience and connections. Try to find a generalist, someone who can objectively assist you in thinking through options, advantages and disadvantages of different paths. They should also be able to use their connections to recommend the appropriate specialists, including legal and estate planning experts. They might be able to assist you in taking whatever new direction you might be considering.

+ **Create a preferred profile**. Too often, organizations search for candidates, select someone with many of the qualities they want and then make the person fit the need. We always recommend that organizations avoid that path by thinking more about the particulars of their desired future, what the future client base, the community or congregation will look like, and then

> **With a preferred profile in mind, it's much easier to find the right candidates.**

about the strategic qualities needed in the person who will guide and steer this successful endeavor. This type of reverse engineering ensures a more appropriate fit for everyone involved.

With a preferred profile in mind, it's much easier to find the right candidates. This illustration explains how this happens. Once you decide to buy a red Toyota, for example, you begin noticing many other red Toyotas on the road. Those cars were there before; you're only noticing them because now you're tuned into that style. Once you develop a preferred profile for a new leader, the same thing begins happening in your leadership search.

+ **Separate competency and loyalty issues.** It's natural to want to reward someone to whom you feel close. But giving that person the top spot in a succession plan isn't necessarily the best move for the organization. It's important to consider competency above all else; this isn't the time for emotional decisions.

Family businesses make this type of mistake frequently, especially when a parent wants to reward a favorite child. Rather than handing out a reward, focus on selecting the leader with the right qualities. Look for someone with the experience, the wisdom and the prudence to handle the organization's affairs effectively. There are other ways to reward loyalty.

The gospels identify a special relationship between Jesus and the apostle John. In many places, he's referred to as "the disciple whom He loved."[34] John was the only disciple present when Jesus was crucified; Jesus even entrusted his mother to John. Peter was also part of Jesus' inner circle. In contrast to John, he often seemed contentious, created issues for Jesus and even denied his Master three times.

> The wrong successor can undo in two years what has taken twenty years to build.

On the day of Pentecost, however, it wasn't John who was selected as spokesman; Peter got that leadership role. It's as if Jesus was saying, "John, I love you. I trust you with my mother. But to establish my church, I need someone with the boldness to stand up and say, 'You crucified Him! Repent and be baptized—every one of you!'"

We must be careful about surrounding ourselves with *Johns* because we love them while marginalizing *Peters* because they create issues for us. We need a successor with the right competencies, someone who can continue the legacy—not someone whose primary qualification is their love for us. The wrong successor can undo in two years what has taken twenty years to build.

◆ **Plan abandonment.** It's difficult for most entrepreneurs and senior leaders to relinquish the helm. It's even more problematic for those who value centralized control. The right management philosophy can make succession easier. For example, a participatory leadership culture that decentralizes decision-making can prevent problems during the crunch of transitions. An unwillingness to surrender control can have unwanted effects.

In 1997, AT&T's board and CEO were embarrassed when the successor they selected in a high-profile search resigned after only nine months—taking with him a $3.8 million severance package and an additional $22.8 million for earnings lost after leaving his previous company to join the telecom giant. Analysts explained his early departure by citing the incumbent CEO's management style. "For eight of his years as CEO, he refused to name a president with his board's full compliance. . . . Mr. Walter is now the second president to quit in a year. Alex Mandl resigned last summer after Mr. Allen wouldn't designate Mr. Mandl as his heir apparent." [35]

> **It's important to understand the difference between change and transition.**

♦ **Be conscious of subtle messages.** "He's my right-hand man." "When I'm not here, she speaks on my behalf." Simple statements like these can be misunderstood and extrapolated into a future state. Pastors sometimes do this by always choosing to sit with a particular associate. I (Dr. Chand) have seen ministers who unwittingly send messages about who will succeed them. Once everyone is told from the platform that his "son" will be the pastor, it can create false expectations that are difficult to correct.

♦ **Think through change and transitional issues.** In the context of succession, it's important to understand the difference between change and transition. Change is the *external* events that result from a decision or an event. Transition relates to the *internal* emotional, relational, psychological and even financial processing of this change. Grasping these distinctions can aid succession planning. It's rarely the change itself that causes problems; the culprit is typically a lack of transitional planning. Often, leaders spend so much time on the change-related activities that they neglect the critical transitional issues. An effective succession plan must address both.

◆ **Communicate.** Whenever someone leaves, the people who remain are typically only focused on the loss. Because of this, we must work hard to provide some reassurance for those who will receive the news. We should always consider ways to help them make adjustments. For example, we can focus on the successor's qualifications. If necessary, we might want to address any concerns about job security. We need to talk about what's coming next. It's important to consider what can be said to give people a level of comfort in the face of change.

It's especially important to focus on communication when stakeholders and shareholders are involved. How the announcement is made to stakeholders and shareholders—and the context it's put in—will greatly affect their reaction and their confidence in the new leadership.

When transitioning from Beulah Heights University, I (Dr. Chand) held many meetings at various levels to communicate fully about my departure. In each of these sessions, I offered background on the decision-making process and talked specifically about transitional issues that I knew were on people's minds. In addition to introducing my successor, I affirmed and validated both his credentials and his leadership. I also provided information about what my role as chancellor would be and talked about future protocol. I always reserved time for questions and thanked the assembled team for their continued support. We closed every meeting with me praying for blessings upon my successor, Dr. Karanaja.

◆ **If necessary, build a bridge.** Suppose an executive nearing retirement age identified a great candidate with many of the qualities needed in a successor. The only problem is that the successor doesn't quite have sufficient experience. Is he forced to remain on the job until the candidate is ready?

While remaining might be one option, he might also consider bringing in a transitional leader, someone who can bridge the gap until the successor is ready. While this path offers benefits within a family business, the idea is applicable in any organization. "A CEO with talents that complement the owner's can add enormous value to the company and help dad train the next generation of family leadership, developing a much stronger company."[36]

The transitional leader is regarded as a bridge, which is a strategic role. How strategic? Keep in mind that in wartime, invaders often demolish bridges to stop the flow of people and supplies.

Important transitional leaders are described in the Bible. Ruth was a bridge. When Naomi connected Ruth to Boaz, it was another link in the lineage of Jesus. While there's a great deal of information about Abraham and Jacob, comparatively little is said about Isaac. His name means laughter; in some ways, he's regarded as a joke. There was no serious focus to his life. The promise was given to Abraham and the nation was born in Jacob. His major purpose was to serve as a bridge between two generations.

Final Perspectives

"Life is pleasant. Death is peaceful," wrote the novelist Issac Asimov. "It's the transition that's troublesome." The same might be said of succession planning. There are only two ways to avoid trouble:

be in denial or be finished with the task. If you're not in one of those places, you're trying to figure out the next step.

Succession planning is a complex process. In order to solve the many related issues, we have to come to a better understanding of the problem. Once we've thoroughly dissected it, we are ready to begin moving forward. In his book, *Managing Transitions: Making the Most of Change,* noted change and transition expert William Bridges says that 90 percent of a leader's efforts should be spent on selling the problem and understanding what is not working.

Bridges' advice is the reason we've taken time to examine what's worked and what hasn't. Before we can create and implement an effective succession plan, it's critical to consider the many aspects of the journey that we're facing. While there are no guarantees, adequate preparation can help us navigate this road successfully.

Selecting and Developing Successors

Effective organizations and companies have moved far beyond seeing succession as a one-time event that's aimed only at replacing an

> **Succession planning is about building the organization's future.**

aging executive. Instead, they've made succession a key organizational process on a par with sales, stakeholder meetings and strategic planning.

Many of America's most-admired companies—GE, Bank of America, Johnson & Johnson, McDonald's and others—have already invested much time, energy and money in this key area. Succession planning, they realize, is about building the organization's future. Selecting and developing the right people is the critical linchpin in that process. Against the background of today's graying executive ranks, they understand that advancing an organization's competitive advantage and effectiveness is all about selecting and developing successors.

Our organizations need to experience a profound change in focus about succession planning. We must make the critical connection between organizational success and leadership sustainability. In the words of one veteran in succession planning, "Acquiring and retaining the right leaders has become every bit as vital as having the right business strategy."[37]

This chapter is designed to help you consider how your organization can begin finding and growing the right leaders. If you're already involved in succession planning, it will expose you to new ideas, expand your thinking, or serve as a reminder. Since real leadership is about developing others, we also provide thoughts and strategies for building your own leadership-development process, regardless of the size and budget of your organization.

> **Advancing an organization's competitive advantage and effectiveness is all about selecting and developing successors.**

Many of the examples that you'll find here might be from organizations very different from yours, in terms of their size, scope and mission. We believe there's great value in evaluating ideas and strategies from paradigms that are significantly different. Regardless of their origins, the insights that you gain are equally applicable in sacred or secular organizations.

Selecting a Successor

In this section, we'll address a number of issues that commonly arise concerning successor selection, including:

- The debate over internal versus external candidates
- Evaluating tangible and intangible qualities

- Considerations for family-owned businesses
- Thoughts about one versus many replacements
- Bridging generational style issues
- Successor naming considerations

Internal versus external candidates. One of the most commonly debated issues in leadership succession is whether there's a significant advantage to selecting an internal or an external candidate. There are convincing arguments and downsides on both sides.

The daily headlines routinely tell us about large corporations filling their empty CEO slots with outsiders. There's no shortage of examples: Ford hired Alan Mulally, a former Boeing exec; IBM hired Lou Gerstner away from AMEX, while Lee Iacocca came to Chrysler from Ford.

Outsiders bring a fresh perspective to an organization, whether it's a church, a non-profit organization, or a multi-national corporation. It's no surprise that troubled organizations in need of a turnaround tend to favor external leaders. That's why approximately one-third of the S&P 500 companies have imported their CEOs.

> **Cultural compatibility can be the difference between success and failure.**

However, if some critical talents are out-of-balance, an outsider can quickly become a disadvantage. In some cases, ignorance about local traditions and the importance of a strong organizational culture can become serious liabilities. How serious is sensitivity to cultural issues? A mismatch with the organizational culture is widely regarded to be the cause of Carly Fiorina's high-profile departure from computer-maker Hewlett-Packard. This can often be the cause of departures in churches and in other organizations.

Veterans in succession planning urge us to pay careful attention to our organizational culture. "I feel very strongly that any succession must support an organization's beliefs, values, and strategies," says Jack Michaels, CEO of Snap-On Inc. "Boards need to clearly articulate both the culture and values of the corporations in any succession, and decide if they want to maintain them. If they do, then that has got to be a part of the skill set and attributes that the next CEO must bring to the job."[38]

Cultural compatibility can be the difference between success and failure. Boards that rely on external candidates risk hiring someone with no knowledge of the organization's culture. Insiders tend to have more successful track records, says Richard Teerlink, former CEO and chairman of Harley-Davidson, Inc. "In the most successful successions I've seen, the candidate came from the same culture and was able to build on that culture," he says.[39]

At Bronner Brothers, our higher-level executives are family members. Before we bring anyone else into the upper levels of management, we assess how much they grasp our culture and understand who we are. We look for discernment, which deals with the motives behind an action. It isn't necessary for them to be born with our DNA if they have sharp minds and their values are in line with ours. Sometimes, there are cases in family businesses where there's a closer kinship with someone who shares your values than someone who's actually of your own blood.

> A capable leader with significant abilities may be unwilling to wait on the sidelines.

Cultural continuity is only one advantage provided by insiders. They're also cited for better long-term performance. While CEOs brought in from the outside have created higher returns in the first two years, it's the insiders who did better for shareholders over the long haul.[40]

Outsiders aren't the only ones who can turn a troubled organization around. Insiders who understand how an organization works can also be dynamic change agents. For example, Xerox insider Anne Mulcahy started her career with the company in 1976 as a sales rep. Now the company's CEO and chairwoman, she's credited with reviving the business by drawing on her experience and connections within the firm.

Finding a talented insider can be problematic, however. A capable leader with significant abilities may be unwilling to wait on the sidelines. Losing potential candidates reduces our pool of available talent. In addition, internal candidates who are known quantities are somehow perceived as less capable than external ones. It's also not uncommon for

> **Finding an "inside outsider" is one solution that sidesteps the associated downsides of either pole.**

executive search firms to favor external candidates for CEO slots and other high-profile positions. Church boards can find an outsider more intriguing simply because they're unfamiliar territory.

Avoiding the downsides of inside and outside candidates requires time, consideration and investigation. A hastily planned succession can result in the crowning of an outsider who is hobbled by cultural or industry ignorance or "an insider who knows the business but can't lead."[41]

Finding an "inside outsider" is one solution that sidesteps the associated downsides of either pole. Joseph Bower, author of *The CEO Within: Why Inside Outsiders Are the Key to Succession Planning*, describes the solution, "The best leaders are people from inside the company who somehow have maintained enough detachment from the local traditions, ideologies, and shibboleths that they have retained the objectivity of an outsider."[42] According to Bower, the right candidate merges an intimate understanding of our processes and people with a firm grasp of the new world that the organization is entering, thus producing a winning combination.

Tangible and intangible qualities. Typically, evaluating potential candidates involves references and resumes. We suggest developing a sketch of where the organization should be in five to ten years and then identifying candidates with the skills needed to get it there.

> **We hire people for what they can do, but we fire them for who they are.**

Some organizations ask candidates to write a white paper or strategy statement describing their approach to leading the organization.

Despite all the time we spend evaluating tangible qualities, these characteristics don't really reveal much about the person. How much can we realistically expect to learn from a professionally written resume? In the end, it's the intangible qualities—interpersonal skills, conflict resolution, family life, and humility—that are important. Ignore these intangible qualities and they'll come back to bite you.

By looking for important intangible qualities, we can get an early indication of how a person will really perform. To discern intangibles, try placing people into a variety of environments, in addition to the regular interview sessions. Observe how they interact over a weekend, while with family, at a reception or at a baseball game.

Remember that we hire people for what they can do, but we fire them for who they are. It's the intangibles that make up who they are. Attitudes and mindsets aren't qualities that you can discover with a written test; you have to rely upon an intuitive hunch.

Family-owned business considerations. When the board of directors share the same parents or the principals are a husband-wife team, somewhat different considerations apply. Here, decisions about succession can be complicated by emotional factors that aren't present in other companies and organizations.

Sometimes, there are issues of competency. Some say that two-thirds of all family businesses don't require family members to meet minimum qualifications or have related experience before coming to work. More than half of all family-owned companies also lack a written strategic plan.[43]

Even in family businesses that don't conduct business this informally, it's not uncommon to feel an emotional obligation to take care of someone. This can be especially true when a family member insists on having a certain role but lacks certain competencies or won't pursue the necessary qualifications. In these situations, the bottom line has to be doing what's necessary to keep the company effective for the long run. It can't become a popularity contest; it has to be about ensuring competency.

At Bronner Brothers, we've had to remind ourselves that we're competing against some brilliant minds. We have to meet or beat what other companies are producing. If a family member in an important role isn't contributing, consider shifting them somewhere they will do the least amount of damage.

When it comes to succession in higher-level positions, remember that it's best not to force a role on anyone. Be sure to determine if the person that you're considering wants a particular responsibility. You don't want to be surprised after you've put them into a key position by discovering that they have other dreams or simply took the job out of obligation. Also be certain that they either have the necessary qualifications or are willing to pursue them. And make sure that they share your vision and values.

One versus many successors. Warren Buffet has already selected a replacement for his CEO position at Berkshire Hathaway, his widely respected conglomerate. The company's 2007 annual report mentioned that he was still searching for a chief investment officer. In the report, Buffet praised the talents and qualities of an associate who managed the investments of the company's GEICO insurance subsidiary and added, "We need to find a younger person or two made of the same stuff."

Buffet's openness to dividing his responsibilities among multiple replacements is rare. Naming multiple successors is not a path that's trouble free. Jesus summarized the problem when He said, "No one can serve two masters. Either he will hate the one and love the other, or he will be devoted to the one and despise the other."[44]

A workable solution has to include clear roles and responsibilities. Problems will arise when that clarity is missing. For example, when Vladimir Putin stepped aside as Russian president recently, his ally Dmitry Medvedev became his successor. Putin didn't disappear, however; he became Russian prime minister, causing newspapers and diplomats to wonder who was really leading the country.

The Russian people seemed equally wary of Putin's action. "Though Russia's state emblem is a double-headed eagle, history has taught its people to view two-headed power as a monster."[45]

An editorial in *The Wall Street Journal* summarized the Russian succession problem. "In planning this transition, the new prime minister—and still the pre-eminent leader in the country—succeeded in preserving political continuity in the short term. But he has manifestly failed to create a stable political system."[46]

Naming multiple successors is not always an unworkable solution, however. It can be appropriate in cases where it's difficult to find the necessary talents in one person. One of my brothers (Dr. Bronner) is multi-talented. He's the president of his own company, a marketing expert, as well as an extremely talented chemist. Finding a single replacement for him is going to be a challenge.

> **If we're only looking for people like us we may be limiting the future growth of the organization.**

My brother's succession plan will likely have to consider the need for finding two or three different people. In each case, the roles will have to be clear. He'll need a chief marketing officer, a lead chemist, as well as a chief executive. In this case, the roles are diversified enough that conflicts can be avoided. In cases where it's not as clear-cut, it's important to clearly state that there's only one person in charge—one president, one senior pastor or one chief executive.

In some cases, organizations do this by having leaders split their focus between domestic and international business, for example. Churches can do it by differentiating between pastors with a gift in administration and those with a gift in preaching. In this last example, the church elders would need to decide which pastor is going to be the lead pastor.

Generational styles. The communication gaps among the generations currently in our workforce continue providing challenges. We have Baby Boomers, Baby Busters, Generation X people, and Generation Y individuals. Baby Boomers tend to be workaholics.

In some cases, they have problems with expectations from the other generations who appear to want special treatment. Human resources organizations are having difficulty in getting everyone to collaborate successfully.

We've witnessed 60-year old incumbents selecting 48-year old successors. Potentially, that's a problem. Some of these incumbents are picking people who are like them, who represent the closest thing they can find to their comfort zone. This misses the point.

Succession is always about planning the organization's future. In the future, everyone is leaving their respective comfort zones. The future is about change. It's about everyone expanding our circles and our frames of reference. If we're only looking for people like us—in terms of our generation or some other criteria—we may be limiting the future growth of the organization.

Regardless of the type of organization, selecting successful candidates must be a process that's closely integrated with succession planning. Finding an appropriate successor involves always wearing your "candidate selection" hat.

This constant vigilance can provide a number of advantages:

- Watching for potential leaders can provide a longer list of candidates.
- Having a number of choices increases your chances of identifying the right person.
- A longer lead time also means that the organization can pay more attention to developing candidates, which increases their suitability.
- Selecting leadership candidates early offers increased opportunities to evaluate them and offer additional developmental opportunities.

Successor naming considerations. In most cases, you'll either want to recommend someone as your successor or you'll find that person will already be named, perhaps by the board. Each of these situations requires a slightly different focus.

> **Every leader has a responsibility to develop those who can move the organization forward.**

If you're going to recommend someone for the position, realize that you're putting a sizeable amount of your "relational equity" at stake. Your relationship with the organization may be put at risk for a number of different reasons:

- People may simply disagree with your choice.
- There may be one or more people favoring another candidate, whether another person is named or is yet unnamed.
- Particularly in churches, your departure might be perceived as a broken promise, simply because people never expected that you'd leave.
- There might be feelings of abandonment associated with your departure.

Regardless of the reason behind the risk, it's important to understand that it's *you*—not the nominee—that's being placed on probation while everyone waits to see the results produced. If your successor does well, those who accepted your recommendation get the credit. However, if your nominee doesn't work out, you should be prepared to take the blame. Also, depending on the degree of risk, recognize that even though you've made your recommendation, this person might never be accepted. Remember, relay races are won or lost on the passing of the baton.

If you're in a situation where a successor is already named, it's important for you to develop your strategic phase-out plan to ensure a proper handoff of responsibilities. We've illustrated the workings of this plan using the following diagram.

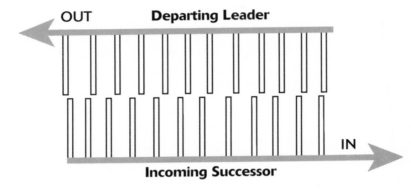

Each line represents a "cog" in the inner workings of the succession process. Each time the cogs on these lines intersect, you're moving one step closer to your final transition from the organization. It's important for each cog to have its own well-defined and well-communicated plan for transferring responsibility. In each case, it's also important that you communicate the distance between each of the cogs—which represents the timeline—and to delineate the overall timeframe for the succession process.

It's possible that each cog will have its own separate stakeholders. This will mean that you'll have to consider different questions, different interests, different agendas and provide different responses to address these varying concerns.

As you move closer to the end of the transition, the interactions become more intense for everyone involved. Your successor and the succession team that remain in the organization will begin feeling the stress of new responsibilities, the incumbent starts recognizing the reality of their approaching departure, and the stakeholders begin the process of releasing one leader while also embracing another.

Developing Leadership Candidates

Greek mythology tells the story of a goddess who sprang fully-grown and armed for battle from her father's head. Wanting to find a successor who is complete in every way is an organizational myth with striking similarities to this ancient Greek fable. In this fast-food world, we shouldn't expect to find a made-to-order successor. Even if we found someone with the right qualifications, some development would likely be necessary.

As this popular quote from Jack Welch reminds us, overseeing the development of others is a necessary part of leadership. "Before you become a leader, success is all about growing yourself. After you become a leader, success is about growing others." Every leader has a responsibility to develop those who can move the organization forward.

> **Leadership development can keep any organization from losing talented people.**

Having a leadership-development focus is an effective method for growing the type of successors your organization needs. A well-designed internal program becomes an incubator for precisely the types of leadership qualities that you require.

Any organization with a reputation for developing leaders gains a number of benefits. Companies with highly regarded development programs typically have an easier time attracting and hiring promising talent. Don't underestimate how attractive a development program can be to potential hires. Attracting new talent is precisely the reason that GE has begun sending high-potential employees to their leadership development center much earlier in their careers. One GE executive told *Fortune* that the program is a "strong selling point" to high-performing young talent.[47]

"Companies that provide people with opportunities to learn and grow become talent magnets, drawing scarce talent in droves," says Robert Gandossy, from the human-resources firm Hewitt, which worked with *Fortune* on a recent study of world-class leadership development programs.

Dynamic leadership development programs—like the ones at GE and at Procter & Gamble—have a proven track record for attracting talent. Graduates of the P&G program have filled CEO slots at nearly 200 companies worldwide. The list of executives nurtured by P&G include GE's Jeff Immelt, 3M's Jim McNerney, eBay's Meg Whitman, Intuit's Steve Cook, Steve Ballmer of Microsoft, and Steve Case of AOL.

> **Developing human capital doesn't necessarily require a substantial investment of financial capital.**

In addition to helping recruit and develop potential successors, leadership development can keep any organization from losing talented people. New employees at Capital One Financial consistently cited development opportunities as one of the top-three reasons they remained at the credit-card company.

The development programs that keep leaders, managers and employees engaged with an organization can also strengthen the bottom line. One Gallup study demonstrated that organizations with engaged workforces have significantly higher levels of customer satisfaction and financial results.[48]

Developing human capital doesn't necessarily require a substantial investment of financial capital. There are ways that any organization—regardless of its size or its budget—can begin developing its own pipeline of succession candidates.

We always encourage senior leaders on all levels to focus on increasing the problem-solving skills of their leadership teams. You can use the issues and problems that they're facing in their current positions to challenge them to grow to the next level. For example, a large church with its own parking-lot attendants can focus on developing skills in dealing with cantankerous people who insist on parking where they want. By helping the attendants—and the leaders responsible for this job—to think through these problems, we're really focusing on people skills, conflict resolution and eliminating chaos. The leaders responsible for these areas can apply the same thinking to dealing with issues facing the ushers, nursery workers and other areas in a church.

> **Measure a leader's effectiveness and worth to the organization based on their ability to solve problems.**

We should also work with leaders on developing the ability to anticipate certain issues. We challenge our people to assume that they will encounter resistance, to consider the negative forces that might work against them. We encourage them to prepare for these situations, to find ways to respond in advance of these events. Observing people as they strategize about these situations reveals a lot about their capabilities. Leaders have to be effective problem solvers. We measure a leader's effectiveness and worth to the organization based on their ability to solve problems. Watching them respond to hypothetical problems shows me how they might think in the midst of a storm.

Broadening people beyond their current positions and functions is another simple and inexpensive way to develop leaders. Cross-training is a valuable and frequently overlooked strategy that can help leaders to grasp the big picture about an organization and its world. Why not consider taking leaders out of their comfort zones by exposing them to unfamiliar areas? Provide cross-training that exposes the financial people to marketing, or the marketing people to information technology, for example. The point is not to make them uncomfortable, but to broaden their horizons and their potential.

> **Many report that they're enjoying the development activities more than they're enjoying preaching.**

One of the co-chairmen of Harvard Business School's program for high-potential leaders, Das Narayandas, describes what happens to leaders who fail to develop this critical multifaceted outlook. "If they are not trained the right way, they can spend the next twenty years building deeper and deeper skills in a narrow aspect."[49]

Any development program assumes that the organization has some idea about the qualities and competencies that it values. If you haven't already, describe those important qualities and attributes. From there, find ways to provide the necessary training and development opportunities. Many organizations employ some method of assessing where their leaders are in relation to important attributes. This enables them to personalize development.

Growing and developing others is not solely the work of a human resources department. It's vital for leaders from the Baby Boomer generation to realize this and to become more intentional about developing others. Whenever I (Dr. Chand) work with pastors and other organizational leaders, I realize how many of us were not apprenticed. It's rare that I find someone that was purposefully and closely mentored.

That situation is changing in many top companies, where senior leaders are increasingly more involved in leadership development. The CEO at McDonald's—Jim Skinner—personally reviews the development progress of the company's top 200 candidates. At GE, Jeff Immelt monitors the progress of the top 600 leaders. Other executives report that they devote 50 percent of their time to people issues. Some corporations are encouraging these activities by attaching a percentage of their CEO's compensation to successful leadership development.[50]

Boards are also involved in the development of potential successors. Their focus is on ensuring that their organizations have more than enough candidates, which offers them choices when it's time to actually select the next pastor or CEO. Board members want regular updates on how candidates are being prepared. They want to know about plans to expand their responsibilities to provide needed experiences, find out about their delegation and management skills, and get feedback on their leadership skills. It's also not uncommon for board members to visit a church, branch or a location run by a high-level candidate to get a first-hand look at them in operation.

> **You achieve greater impact by investing more time in smaller groups of people.**

Adopting the purposeful development models that we observe in top corporations is not out of any organization's reach. We always tell senior leaders that the first step is to realize that we must find ways to give away what we were never given, to provide a gift to the next generation of leaders. Since we tend to teach like we were taught, just having that realization is vital. From there, we can begin to take the necessary steps.

When I (Dr. Chand) am guiding a senior pastor or another leader in developing others, I simplify the task for them. I start by asking them to create a list of twelve things they want their leadership team to understand. Once the list is developed, we prioritize the items.

That list becomes a twelve-month development schedule. The senior leader then begins considering the first month's material and looking toward gathering their leadership team together. While many of them are pastors with impressive preaching experience, it's not uncommon for them to be a bit nervous. It's as though they're riding a bike for the first time; when I break it down for them in this way, I'm providing the training wheels. After they introduce the overview of the twelve items and deliver the first session to their team, we evaluate how it went. Then, they get busy working on the next month's development session.

By about the fourth month, it starts flowing fairly well. They typically have fallen into a rhythm by then. When I ask them about their progress, most of them are excited. Many report that they're enjoying the development activities more than they're enjoying preaching. At about the sixth or seventh

> **Find someone who's serious because once your time is wasted, you'll never get it back.**

month, these leaders are beginning to discover who are the eagles in their team. As they are teaching, they can often see it on their faces.

By the sixth month, I'm providing them with the necessary guidance and support needed for the next step, which is having their senior leaders cascade the same material to their teams. We can't do that in the beginning of this process; we first have to get a few months of experience.

These development steps actually follow a Biblical pattern. Joshua worked with the leaders, who told the officers, and the officers told the congregation.[51] Jesus had the multitudes, developed the twelve disciples, and was closely mentoring three of them. Likewise, the higher your leadership position, the fewer people you can mentor directly. You achieve greater impact by investing more time in smaller groups of people.

> **All good leaders recognize their limitations.**

Formal development is not sufficient. It's critical that we also begin mentoring one or more leaders to fully develop competent successors. Mentoring is different from development because it provides a level of accessibility between a senior leader and a protégé. It offers the opportunity for more individualized conversations that can be more personalized than group sessions.

Top organizations are realizing that they cannot rely completely upon classroom training, regardless of how stellar these training sessions might be. Many are beginning to rely more on this formula: "About two-thirds of leadership development comes from job experience, about one-third from mentoring and coaching, and a smidgen from classroom training."[52]

At Natura, Brazil's largest cosmetics company, top leaders might spend three to six months shadowing a high-level executive. CEOs who have been blessed with mentors praise the effect that it's had on them. "I am here today in part due to a handful of people who, before it was in vogue, provided coaching and mentoring to me early in my career," said Whirlpool CEO Jeff Fettig. "They helped me to develop."[53]

Our organizations have high-potential leaders—including our successors—who need to be mentored. Many of them are looking for someone to take an interest in them, to help them to develop to the next stage.

It's important to know what's involved in mentoring and what qualities to look for in a protégé. In my book *Pass The Baton*, I (Dr. Bronner) describe important considerations on both sides of this relationship. It's vital for the mentor to define the parameters of the mentoring relationship. They shouldn't have to worry about getting phone calls at home if they don't want them. They should begin by actually setting the limits on the relationship. This can include what mode of contact they prefer, whether email is appropriate, and what hours they'll take phone calls.

> **Every leadership development program must challenge and inspire leaders to achieve new limits and push beyond their boundaries.**

They should also find a way to sensitively help the protégé to understand that they're providing developmental coaching. They're not providing monetary loans, which can quickly ruin the relationship, or acting as a caretaker. If they find someone who needs caretaking, it's a sign that this person is not ready to be mentored.

We will all encounter people that aren't ready yet. Because they're not committed to the process, we shouldn't invest our time in them. When people who are not fully committed ask for your time, tell them that you cannot commit yourself to anyone who is less than fully committed. If a potential protégé isn't hungry enough to pursue the relationship, they don't respect your wisdom and they won't respect your time. Find someone who's serious because once your time is wasted, you'll never get it back.

There has to be a mutual searching and readiness on both sides.

In the words of the old Chinese proverb, "When the student is ready the teacher will appear." Both the mentor and the protégé must be at a point in their lives and their careers where they're ready for this sort of relationship. In some cases, a leader won't seek a mentor until they realize some deficiency in themselves. Until something creates a need in them, most people don't accept someone coming into their lives to develop them in this way. They begin to realize that they need help and develop the very necessary quality of a teachable heart. All good leaders recognize their limitations.

Once a protégé realizes their limits, they may begin searching for someone who has been to places that they have not, someone with the vision to see what's needed, someone to guide them along the path that they're traveling. A mentor may begin to realize how different their life might have been if they'd had personal guidance. They look back and wish they had someone to provide guidance and answer tough questions early in their career. The mentor is now in a position to help a pastor just beginning a church, for example. He's ready to provide counsel and pour years of wisdom into that expectant young leader. As you begin working together with a protégé, perhaps you'll realize that you've found your successor.

General Electric calls its leadership development program "Inspirational Leadership." That's an appropriate mission statement for any leadership development activity. Every leadership development program must challenge and inspire leaders to achieve new limits and push beyond their boundaries.

When our successors are experienced in moving forward in their own leadership journeys, they're ready to provide this level of visionary leadership to our churches, our organizations and our companies. Once they have been developed and challenged, they're ready to begin creating the future.

Making a Graceful Exit

A friend of ours left a ministerial position to write full-time. Working out of his home meant he no longer had to travel to his office at the church everyday. Some habits were hard to break, however. Every morning, he rose at the same time, put on a suit and went downstairs to his computer.

> **Walking away is no easy task.**

That story summarizes some of the awkwardness surrounding succession planning. Part of the planning process must involve dealing with habits we've practiced for decades and identities that provided us a large measure of our self-worth. Walking away is no easy task. Even if we've planned for retirement, most of our work surrounding our succession or retirement planning has likely focused only on building a financial nest egg. Most retirement planning materials spend little time on the internal transitions we must navigate.

Any successful transition must involve planning the next steps in our personal journey and assisting whoever succeeds us. It also means confronting whatever anxieties we might have, examining what really motivates us and considering the source of our self-image. Providing considerations and ideas about these personal issues is the focus of this chapter.

Common Transitional Issues

"The hardest thing," according to one expert in entrepreneurial business, "is figuring out how to let go."[54]

It doesn't matter how big or how influential your organization might be, navigating the next step in your transition is going to create some anxiety. It's best to be prepared to confront the inevitable emotions.

When Bill Gates announced his departure from Microsoft for a full-time role running his charitable foundation, his separation anxiety was evident. Gates told *Fortune* that he got choked up while rehearsing his speech prior to the press conference for his announcement. He worried about leaving the company he founded for something new. "I don't even know what it's going to be like," he said. "I'm taking a risk here that I'm going to miss it very badly."[55]

> **"The hardest thing is figuring out how to let go."**

One of the world's richest men also expressed concern about leaving the security of Microsoft for a new endeavor. "I don't know what it's going to feel like not to come in every day and work 10 hours," he said. "I have a sense of what it's like to do foundation work because I've squeezed it in part time. . . . It might take me a year and a half to get used to my role. That's a little bit of an unknown now."[56]

Considering a move away from a high-level leadership role is disconcerting. We may feel as though we're disconnecting from a large piece of our everyday existence and identity. As we depart, we may also feel like we're leaving behind a huge chunk of our status and our self-worth. It's an awkward but unavoidable transition.

Certainly, we can deny or prolong the inevitable day of departure. Media mogul Sumner Redstone, the chairman of Viacom, was 82 years old when he decided to relinquish his CEO role after the company split into two entities. Redstone advised Michael Eisner not to even consider leaving his position as Disney's CEO, despite the board's plans to oust him. "Once you've had this kind of power Michael, let's face it, nobody wants to give it up." Redstone confirmed his attachment to the throne in subsequent comments to *Fortune*, "My advice in succession is, 'Don't go. Stay!' "[57]

> **Even when you're no longer a pastor, there are talents and gifts that remain part of your nature and your essence.**

An attachment to the privileges that accompany our positions will certainly occur. When I (Dr. Chand) chose to leave my role as college president, I had to make certain adjustments. I no longer had that office or the assistant that made my work easier. One day, I was the college president. The next day, I had to start over again as "Sam." But it was a choice.

George Barna cites the attachment to power as a major reason for the lack of succession planning among Baby Boomers. "We love power," he writes. "Whether it is because of an unhealthy desire for control, a reasonable concern about maintaining quality, a sense of exhilaration received from making pressure-packed, life-changing decisions or due to other motivations, Boomers revel in power. The sad result is that most Boomers—even those in the pastorate or in voluntary, lay-leadership positions in churches—have no intention of lovingly handing the baton to Baby Busters."[58]

This attachment to power, however, is often a symptom of another issue. While it's more observable among men, it's not uncommon for any leader to define success solely by professional accomplishments. Rabbi Shmuley Boteach describes the attachment

> **Making a transition can free us to consider our dreams.**

to power as one of the symptoms of male self-esteem issues in his book, *The Broken American Male and How to Fix Him.*

Citing both Michael Jackson and Bill Clinton as examples, Boteach says that too many men get the majority of their self-esteem from externals. Jackson's value came from how many albums he sold, while Clinton's came from living in the spotlight. Rather than attaching value to who they are, they became performance oriented, Boteach says.

"The broken American male lives to impress other people," he says. "He doesn't know how to be. He only knows how to perform. When he isn't working, he feels he isn't existing. . . . He is trained to be a lifelong competitor."[59]

Successfully navigating our personal transitions involves get-

> **Facing ourselves is a necessary part of successful succession planning.**

ting in touch with our values and our motivations instead of focusing on externals. It means considering our dreams and identifying precisely who we are. In the end, we can quit a posi-

tion but we cannot quit who we are. A mover-and-shaker type is going to continue directing traffic and organizing even if they leave a CEO or senior leadership slot to volunteer somewhere.

There are certain things that are part of who you are. Even when you're no longer a pastor, there are talents and gifts that remain part of your nature and your essence. Each of us must find ways to realize what those things are. We must ask ourselves: What would we continue doing even after we relinquish this role or position? Those things are part of who we are. Wherever we are, we will always express those values and those gifts.

When I (Dr. Bronner) consider my eventual transition from pastoring, I know that there are many things about this role that I'll continue doing. I look forward to being free from the support-related tasks, which are the very things that cause burnout among pastors. I am looking forward to just being able to do what I love. Making a transition can free us to consider our dreams.

Succession planning provides us with an opportunity to face ourselves. We have the privilege of confronting ourselves apart from our everyday work and considering what's important to us. While she describes this inner scrutiny in terms

> It's about finding our joy and making it our job.

of retirement planning, Betsy Kyte Newman expresses this necessary analysis in her book *Retirement as a Career*.

"The changes that retirement brings can either arrest our spiritual and psychological development or move us to new personal discoveries and a reintegration of ourselves. In retirement, we face ourselves without the burdens and distractions of work; if we stay with the journey, and the fear and pain it brings, we can discover a source of positive power, the path of our true purpose, and the real passion of our lives."[60]

> Most of the senior pastors that we know desire to mentor and pour themselves into other pastors and leaders.

Facing ourselves is a necessary part of successful succession planning. Bill Gates said that his own transition was the result of a decision to "reorganize" his personal priorities, a process that involved "much soul searching." It's about continuing our journey toward a balanced existence. Finding that elusive balance is not about scheduling every minute of every day; it's about discovering and emphasizing what we value. It's about finding our joy and making it our job.

> **Large speaking venues may be attractive, but they do not have the same dynamic effect as developing a small group of others.**

Most of the senior pastors that we know desire to mentor and pour themselves into other pastors and leaders. Because their schedules don't allow much room for this, they can rarely make it happen. It only seems to occur when they're invited to speak in other churches or asked to address a leadership conference. The more intentional development of other leaders just doesn't happen in the manner that they'd like. If you're one of these pastors, remember that while large speaking venues may be attractive, they do not have the same dynamic effect as developing a small group of others. We encourage you not to let "the job"—the things that you have to do—keep you from getting joy from the things that you want to do.

Navigating a New Transition

Today's health-care advances have pushed the average life expectancy years to 77 years. That's a significant jump from the 1935 average of 61 years.[61] This increased life expectancy is changing how people think about those years and prompting new thoughts about how to spend that time.

No longer is "retirement" equated with being put out to pasture and endless days of fishing or golfing. Changes in thinking about the retirement years offer opportunities to forge new paths as we conduct our succession planning. As one article in *Smart-*

Money magazine put it, "For a growing number of people in their 50s and 60s, retirement has become a time to reinvent themselves."[62]

Here are some of the significant changes in thinking about retirement.[63]

> **"For us, this time is an opening up. In my parents' generation, it was a closing down."**

- Surveys show that Boomers plan to continue working, cycling between periods of work and leisure to create a new retirement model.
- Most intend to leave their current role when they're 64 and launch into a completely new endeavor.
- Most say that cycling between work and leisure periods is the ideal work arrangement (42 percent).
- Large percentages of Boomers plan to pursue part-time work (16 percent), start a business (13 percent), or continue working full-time (6 percent). Only 17 percent hope they'll never work again.
- It's not financial gain that's motivating this interest in work. More than 65 percent cite the desire for mental stimulation and continued challenges. Only 37 percent indicated they needed or wanted the money.

One 60-year old psychologist summed up the meaning of today's different view of the retirement years. "For us, this time is an opening up. In my parents' generation, it was a closing down."[64]

Leaving our current position—by itself—will seem negative unless we are transitioning into some other activity that fully engages our attention. Like Bill Gates—who moved from Microsoft to his foundation—we need some other focus. My dad (Dr. Bronner) had another attractive opportunity, which I'm sure made it easier for him to leave the business to his sons. He had purchased a spa and motel on 700 acres of land in Alabama. He began to shift his attention to developing and transforming that business. Dad knew that his mind would need something to do when he left his daily role in the family business. He wanted to give us freedom and he needed something to keep himself occupied. All of us need to transfer our creativity, our leadership and vision to something else that gives us significance.

> **It's especially necessary for founders and entrepreneurs to have another focus. If they don't, it's going to be harder for them to keep from interfering.**

It's especially necessary for founders and entrepreneurs to have another focus. If they don't, it's going to be harder for them to keep from interfering. Having too much idle time may cause them to worry that their successors are making mistakes that will destroy what they've built. Working on something else that commands your attention, something that gives you a sense of renewed purpose, fulfillment and meaning will be good for you and for your successor.

Moving forward with a succession plan must involve identifying our motivations and taking some time to tune into our dreams. Once we've spent time planning the organization's future, we must spend time planning our own future. Answering some simple questions can make it easier to develop a clear plan for our lives before stepping down. For example:

- What would I do if weren't running this organization?
- What would I like to accomplish in the next 10 years?
- What would I like to change about my life?
- Do I want to remain close to the work, perhaps in a consulting role?

- How much would I like to travel?
- What volunteer or charity work has always attracted me?

There will be many new opportunities available to us after succession. Developing a plan for our lives as part of our transition planning can help us to take advantage of these new prospects.

Smoothing the Way for a Successor

Planning the organization's future and giving ample thought to our own, aren't the only considerations we must make in succession planning. We must also ensure that we gracefully pass the baton to our successor in a positive, affirming manner. It's crucial that we establish the right tone for this change.

"As an act of Christian stewardship, it is our responsibility to pass on the baton with grace, love, hope, excitement and joy,"[65] writes George Barna. "How does the Lord want you to bless—rather than

"CEOs can stay too long."

bully and block—the generation of leaders who will inevitably replace you? What can you teach them about the heart and character of God through the way you welcome them into leadership?"

What we do and don't do will inevitably send messages throughout the organization. Departing provides us with an opportunity to—as Barna put it—"set the table" for the leader following us.

One of the best ways to set the stage for a successor is by establishing and adhering to a reasonable but definite departure date. "It's important to know when your work is done," Mark Hurd, CEO of Hewlett-Packard told *Fortune* magazine. "CEOs can stay too long."

Sometimes, CEOs and other leaders stay on even after their departure date. I (Dr. Chand) have a friend who succeeded a university president. The former president chose to keep an office at the university. He continued going to his office everyday because of the perks it offered. Unfortunately, the institution had two heads because the former president couldn't sit on his hands and kept getting involved.

It was a situation that was very different from my departure from Beulah Heights. When I drove away from the campus, I knew that my presence could make the transition more difficult for my successor. Even now, years after my departure in December of 2003, I only return when I have an appointment or an invitation. I don't just drop by. I endeavored to do everything possible to give my successor, Dr. Karanja, room to establish his leadership without me lurking around.

> **It's important to establish and maintain strong boundaries after your departure.**

I also established clear boundaries with the people who were on my staff. In my last staff meeting, I said, "Today, I am president. Next week, I will not be a president. You have my email address and you're welcome to communicate with me as a friend. But please understand that I will never discuss college business with you."

It's important to establish and maintain strong boundaries after your departure. Don't allow people to circumvent the new leader. You might even consider letting everyone know that if they send you an email about issues concerning your old position, that you'll be forwarding the message to your successor.

There are situations where it might make sense to remain with the organization, but in another role. This is different from what occurs in large corporations. Unless they also happen to be the board's chairman, once a CEO is replaced, that person typically departs. In smaller organizations and entrepreneurial firms, it's often beneficial for the organization to have the founder around in some well-defined role. In some cases, a departing CEO might remain in a lower-ranking executive role, such as chief-technology officer, for example. It might benefit the church for the founding pastor to remain available as a consultant. For example, I (Dr. Chand) now serve on the university board and as president-emeritus.

When my dad (Dr. Bronner) transitioned the business to his sons, he made himself available in a part-time consulting role, but only when his assistance was requested. This provided us with a real psychological sense of security. We knew that he wasn't threatened by us and we knew that he wanted us to achieve more than he had. By physically moving his office elsewhere, Dad gave us the freedom to make mistakes. He gave us the liberty to foul up big time. Admirably, Dad sat on his hands and would not interfere. He knew that great lessons are often derived from mistakes. When we needed him, he would always be available to help us evaluate a course of action.

When properly planned and implemented, staying connected to the organization might aid a transition. When handled in a phased approach, this method can be especially reassuring to customers, a congregation and other stakeholders. It's

Proper planning prevents poor performance.

crucial, however, that a departing leader's role be very well defined. Proper planning prevents poor performance. It could prove extremely awkward for a new senior pastor or CEO to establish their leadership while their predecessor is still around, or to have their predecessor reporting to them. How you leave is more important than how you came in.

Whether it's appropriate in your situation to depart or to remain connected, it's always important to honor your successor and do whatever you can to help them rise to the task of establishing the organization's future. Find ways to praise their capabilities to those who remain. Look for opportunities to pass along the heartbeat, the culture and the vision that drive the organization to your successor.

"Build bridges," writes George Barna "Allow them to build on the vision in ways that respect the vision but reflect the evolving context. If you have shared God's vision in a way that they too treasure and commit to, then you have done your job. Move on."[66]

Considerations
for Successors

Succession planning may not be a "slam dunk," but this complex process quickly pales in comparison to the uphill climb facing an incoming successor.

After the planning and selection process is concluded, a new incumbent faces the challenges of meeting and exceeding a congregation's expectations, satisfying waiting shareholders or bearing up under the scrutiny of key stakeholders. Filling those proverbial shoes, or making your own tracks, can be daunting.

> **All change
> is a critique of the past.**

If you're succeeding an outgoing leader, you may already know that the bookshelves lack specific guidance for your situation. That's the reason for this chapter—to provide some compass points to help you navigate the many transitions that you'll encounter. We hope to assist you with a list of do's and don'ts—providing you with actions to avoid, as well as those that may help you to prosper.

Actions to Avoid: The *Don't* List

Don't expect things to be the same for you as they were for your predecessor. Even though Moses affirmed Joshua's leadership in the sight of Israel, it's likely that there were people who were still sold on Moses and resistant to the new leader. Some people would be sold on Moses until the day he died. Even then, they likely still had problems with Joshua. Maybe it was for this reason that God took Moses "for a walk" and never brought him back.

If people seem resistant, try not to take it personally. Realize that it's a loyalty issue and that some folks just need more time to adjust to change. You can't expect the same response from people that your predecessor received. Try thinking of your tenure as a bank account. Any bank account requires deposits. In this case, your stakeholders must make the deposits based on their level of trust in you. Getting that account built up takes time. Your predecessor's years of deposits into the account enabled him or her to get the desired responses. Unfortunately, that account was closed when you became the incumbent; you must now establish your own account. In time, your faithful work will yield similar results.

> **Since change that's imposed is change that's opposed, focus on building relationships at first.**

Don't be quick to make changes for which you lack the necessary relational equity. When I (Dr. Bronner) first started pastoring, someone advised me, "Let the changes you make be evolutionary, not revolutionary." This advice is also connected to the "bank account" analogy mentioned in the previous point, the one in which the stakeholders make all of the deposits. If you start disassembling everything that preceded you or initiating too many completely new endeavors, it's going to put everyone into a state of shock. People who are in shock aren't going to be too keen on making the necessary deposits into your account.

Sometimes, incoming successors make promises or attempt to cast an organizational vision that's totally unrealistic in an effort to get people behind them. Without a relevant track record with their people, they're going to have a very difficult time.

> **Resist the pressure to become their carbon copy.**

Incoming leaders must realize that all change is a critique of the past. Even something as seemingly insignificant as painting a wall or moving the pulpit can be misperceived.

In some cases, new leaders begin taking too many drastic actions. Their people find themselves wondering what was wrong with the way things were and why it was necessary to make so many changes. This reaction may also occur with small change—if you unknowingly target the wrong program to begin your improvement efforts.

It's always better to start small. Since change that's imposed is change that's opposed, focus on building relationships at first. It's vital relationships that will provide you with the equity you'll need for successful future efforts. You can make incremental changes, but be sure to balance those endeavors with getting the necessary relational support. Until you do, you may find yourself writing checks that you cannot cash.

Don't think that people are going to view you like they viewed you before you came. Hard as it may be to believe, there are people who may have wanted a different leadership candidate in your spot. Sure, they were courteous and pleasant when they met with you during the selection process, but they may have had other preferences. Don't rush them; give them time to adjust. Sometimes, they may not have been involved in the entire decision-making process; they may have just received an announcement. You likely have had more time to adjust than they have.

Don't try to be your predecessor. Certainly, you should be respectful toward your predecessor, honoring their accomplishments and their character. If you're following a tremendous leader, one who casts a large shadow, it can cause you to feel compelled to live up to their accomplishments or their reputation. Resist the pressure to become their carbon copy.

Don't be afraid to allow your uniqueness to show. You may have to say things like, "I am not here to fill anyone's shoes." (Maybe

> **Acceptance isn't synonymous with arrival.**

you don't need to say it to anyone else but yourself.) Remember that Joshua didn't attempt to fill Moses' shoes. The world didn't need another Moses; they needed a Joshua. Your organization doesn't need another person like your predecessor; they need you.

Recommended Actions: The *Do* List

Honor and celebrate your predecessor. In many cases, the predecessor who left you an organization to lead is loved and revered. Since people are in the process of shifting their loyalties from that leader to you, it serves you well to honor and celebrate him whenever there is opportunity. As you celebrate your predecessor, you make it easier for people to make their transitions.

Exercise patience. Following a founder, a successful entrepreneur or a much-loved senior pastor is no easy task. It requires self-knowledge and patience, diligence and patience, as well as patience and more patience.

> **Now that you've moved into the first chair, everyone else is relating to you in a different way.**

Even at one pastor's ten-year anniversary celebration, many of the congregation's remarks still invoked the memory of the church founder that this pastor succeeded. It took his predecessor's funeral—twelve years into the new pastor's tenure—for one member to begin calling him "pastor."

While these are extreme examples, it's important to remember that acceptance can take time. How quickly a successor is accepted varies with the organization. In many cases, acceptance isn't synonymous with arrival.

"I think you earn the right to be a pastor over time by a series of decisions and acts of pastoral fidelity," Mike Clingenpeel, pastor of River Road Church in Richmond, VA, told *ABP News*. "It's a process that you feel. . . . It's important to realize that just because you hold the title doesn't mean you hold the trust of the people."[67]

It may help if you can acknowledge the grief and loss associated with the change. For example, you might say, "I know that you miss Pastor Wells. In many ways, I wish he were here myself." Be a realist by acknowledging what people are feeling. Offering them understanding can only help you.

Build relationships with people who have the wisdom to give you advice from the organization's past. Create a counsel of trusted advisors, which is sometimes called a "kitchen cabinet." Realize that you need counsel to help you to make good decisions. Then, connect with the right people. Build good relationships with those that have the experience, the wisdom, and the power and influence. When their input helps you to produce favorable results, be sure to give them credit. But don't risk alienating them by blaming them when something doesn't go well; just ask them for input on what might have caused it and how you might remedy any issues.

Take time to understand the shifts within the organization. You may *think* you know the organization inside and out, perhaps because you were there while you were being developed for your new role. But even though you were in the boardroom before, you were in another chair. Now that you've moved into the first chair, everyone else is relating to you in a different way. When you moved, they changed too. Because of this power shift, you have to adjust your understanding of the organization.

Be flexible and not overly sensitive. Some people will insist on being your critics. We encourage you to carefully inspect each criticism for some truth that can help you to grow. There is a shred of truth in everything. If you approach criticism from this standpoint, every critic can actually help you to grow into a better pastor, a better leader, or a better CEO.

GROW continually. The letters in the word GROW can provide an easy way to remember many of the important transitions that you'll have to navigate.

G rasp the organizational culture, as every organization is different.

R espect and honor your predecessor, as well as the local traditions and customs.

O rganize your strategic thinking and planning while you learn about the organization.

W ork at willingness. Be open to criticism, value and seek out the opinions of others.

Keep a journal of your own transition process to give to your successor. Give your successor every advantage. Record what occurs to you, what you observe and how you feel. It's likely that you'll be able to create your personal list of do's and don'ts that you'll be able to pass along. Even after you select someone, they will still have to deal with transitional issues of becoming a successor and growing into that role. Having your thoughts to refer to can help them to create a solid future for the organization.

References

1. "Xerox's dynamic duo" by Betsy Morris, *Fortune*, November 19, 2007.
2. Proverbs 22:3, New Living Translation, Copyright 1996, 2004 by Tyndale Charitable Trust.
3. "Leadership Forecast: A Benchmarking Study" by Paul R. Bernthal & Cichard S. Wellins, HR Benchmark Group, Development Dimensions International, Inc., Nov. 2003.
4. "Succession Planning: Preparing the Next Generation to Lead Your Business" by David C. Hepple, *The Business Monthly*, Aug. 13, 2006.
5. Ibid.
6. Ibid.
7. "Who's next? Getting ready for a transition at the top" by Mark Hrywna, *The Non-Profit Times*, Feb. 1, 2007.
8. "The Leadership Redux" by Elise Walton, *Consulting*, July/Aug. 2006.
9. "Succession Planning: Preparing the Next Generation to Lead Your Business" by David C. Hepple, *The Business Monthly*, Aug. 13, 2006.
10. 2 Kings 13:21
11. "There's Work Left to Do" *Crain's Cleveland Business*, March 12, 2007, volume 28, issue 10.
12. Ibid.
13. Ibid.

14. Cecil Murphey, *Aging is an Attitude*, (Chattanooga, Tennessee: AMG Publishers, 2005), page 9.

15. "That Sucking Sound," *The Leadership Link*, www.growingleaders.com, September 2006.

16. "The Joshua Problem," *The Leadership Link*, www.growingleaders.com, February 2007.

17. "There's Work Left to Do," *Crain's Cleveland Business*, March 12, 2007, volume 28, issue 10.

18. "Family Business" by Jason Stahl, *SmartBusiness Atlanta*, Feb. 2007.

19. "Sweet Smell of Succession" by Daniel Roth, *Fortune*, September 19, 2005.

20. "Prepare Family Members for Business Succession," *AllBusiness*, www.allbusiness.com, retrieved on Sept. 18, 2007.

21. "Sweet Smell of Succession" by Daniel Roth, *Fortune*, September 19, 2005

22. "Ibid.

23. "All in the Family" by Tom Barry, *Atlanta Business Chronicle*, Oct. 15–21, 2004.

24. "Founder Hubris Fuels Corporate Drama" by George Anders, *The Wall Street Journal*, June 4, 2008.

25. Ibid.

26. "You're Fired. Now What?" by Hannah Clark, *Forbes*, Feb. 25, 2007.

27. Ibid.

28. "Why CEOs Are Not Plug-and-Play," *Working Knowledge for Business Leaders*, Harvard Business School, May 29, 2006.

29. Ibid.

30. "Surviving Success: When Founders Must Go," *Working Knowledge for Business Leaders*, Harvard Business School, October 4, 2006.

31. "The Founding CEO's Dilemma: Stay or Go," *Working Knowledge for Business Leaders*, Harvard Business School, August 15, 2005.

32. "CEO Succession: The Case at Ford," *Working Knowledge for Business Leaders*, Harvard Business School, November 22, 2006.

33. "Target's Inner Circle" by Jennifer Reingold, *Fortune*, March 18, 2008.

34. See John 13:23, 19:26, 20:2, 21:7 and 21:20.

35. "AT&T's Walter Quits After Boardroom Rebuff" by John Keller, *The Wall Street Journal*, April 29, 1997.

36. "Who Follows You?" by Bill Lurz, *Professional Builder*, March 1, 2007, v72, issue 3, page 31.

37. "Two top leaders talk succession" by Randall S. Cheloha and Colleen P. O'Neil, *Directors & Boards*, Spring 2007.

38. Ibid.

39. Ibid.

40. "The Leadership Redux" by Elise Walton, *Consulting*, July/August 2006.

41. "Growing CEOs from the Inside" by Sean Silverthorne, *Working Knowledge for Business Leaders*, Harvard Business School, November 14, 2007.

42. Ibid.

43. "Family-to-Family: The Laird Norton Tyee Family Business Survey 2007," http://www.familybusinesssurvey.com/survey/survey.htm, retrieved on June 5, 2007.

44. Matthew 6:24

45. "Russia's Power Couple" by Ivan Krastev, *The Wall Street Journal*, May 16, 2008.

46. Ibid.

47. "How top companies breed stars" by Geoff Colvin, *Fortune*, September 20, 2007.

48. "Leaders developing leaders" by William J. Maxwell, *Human Resource Planning*, December 2006.

49. "Grooming Next-Generation Leaders" by Martha Lagace, *Working Knowledge for Business Leaders*, Harvard Business School, December 18, 2006.

50. "How top companies breed stars" by Geoff Colvin, *Fortune*, September 20, 2007.

51. Joshua 1.

52. "How top companies breed stars" by Geoff Colvin, *Fortune*, September 20, 2007.

53. Ibid.

54. "Success and succession" by Dee Gill, *Crain's Chicago Business*, May 14, 2007.

55. "Bill Gates reboots" by Brent Schlender, *Fortune*, July 13, 2006.

56. Gates to leave day-to-day role at Microsoft" by Amanda Cantrell, CNN Money.com, June 16, 2006.

57. "Retire? No Way!" by Patricia Sellers, *Fortune*, August 22, 2005.

58. "Gracefully Passing the Baton" by George Barna, *Perspectives*, www.barna.org, April 26, 2004.

59. "American men need trip to spiritual repair shop" by John Chadwick, NorthJersey.com, March 13, 2008.

60. Betsy Kyte Newman, *Retirement as a Career* (Praeger Publishers, 2008), p. 154.

61. "Survey Findings," The 2006 Merrill Lynch New Retirement Study, http://askmerrill.ml.com.

62. "The New Retirement" by Karen Hube, *SmartMoney*, September 6. 2005.

63. "Survey Findings," The 2006 Merrill Lynch New Retirement Study, http://askmerrill.ml.com.

64. "Retirement and reinvention go hand in hand with boomers, North Jersey.com, March 2, 2008.

65. "Gracefully Passing the Baton" by George Barna, *Perspectives*, www.barna.org, April 26, 2004.

66. Ibid.

67. "How long before the new pastor really feels part of a church?" by Hannah Elliott, Associated Baptist Press News, August 22, 2007.

About Dr. Samuel R. Chand

Who would have thought, when in 1973 *"student"* Samuel Chand was serving Beulah Heights Bible College (BHBC) as janitor, cook and dishwasher, that he would return in 1989 as *"President"* of the same college! Under his leadership BHBC became the country's largest predominantly African-American Bible school.

Dr. Chand is a former Pastor, college President, Chancellor and now serves as President Emeritus of Beulah Heights University.

In this season of his life, Dr. Chand does *one* thing—Leadership. His singular vision for his life is to **Help Others Succeed.** Dr. Chand develops leaders through:

- Leadership consultations
- Leadership resources—books/CDs
- Leadership speaking.

As a **Dream Releaser** he serves pastors, ministries and businesses as a *Leadership Architect* and *Change Strategist.* Dr. Chand speaks regularly at leadership conferences, churches, corporations, ministerial conferences, seminars and other leadership development opportunities.

Dr. Chand is very involved in a variety of leadership development endeavors.

Dr. Chand . . .

- Consults with businesses and large churches on leadership and capacity enhancing issues
- Named in the top-30 global *Leadership Gurus* list
- Conducts nationwide Leadership Conferences
- Serves on the board of EQUIP (Dr. John Maxwell's Ministry), equipping five million leaders world-wide
- Oversees and leads Bishop Eddie L. Long's leadership development
- Serves on the board of New Birth Christian Academy
- Serves on the board of Beulah Heights University

Dr. Chand has authored and published seven books.

Failure: The Womb of Success with twenty Christian leaders.

FUTURING: Leading your Church into Tomorrow is creating future oriented dialog across the country.

Who's Holding Your Ladder reminds all leaders that the most critical decision they'll make is selecting their leaders.

Who Moved Your Ladder: **Your Next Bold Move**—provides pragmatic guidelines for dealing with transitions in life and leadership.

What's Shakin' Your Ladder: **15 Challenges All Leaders Face** provides ongoing counsel to high-impact leaders.

LADDER*Shifts: New realities—Rapid change—Your destiny.*
Ladder Focus: **Creating, Sustaining, and Enlarging Your BIG Picture** for leaders who desire focus in their ministry with practical know how.

Leaders are using Dr. Chand's books as handbooks worldwide in leadership development.

His educational background includes an honorary Doctor of Divinity from Heritage Bible College, a Master of Arts in Biblical Counseling from Grace Theological Seminary, a Bachelor of Arts in Biblical Education from Beulah Heights University.

Dr. Chand shares his life and love with his wife Brenda, two daughters Rachel & Deborah and granddaughter Adeline.

Being raised in a pastor's home in India has uniquely equipped Dr. Chand to share his passion—that of mentoring, developing and inspiring leaders to break all limits—in ministry and the marketplace.

For further information on
Samuel R. Chand Consulting, Inc.
please visit
www.samchand.com

About Dr. Dale Carnegie Bronner

Dr. Dale Carnegie Bronner is a graduate of Morehouse College, where he finished as the top student in the field of religion. In 1999, Dr. Bronner was inducted in the prestigious Martin Luther King Board of Preachers at Morehouse College. He earned his doctor of ministry degree from Christian Life School of Theology and has an honorary doctor of divinity degree from St. Thomas Christian College.

He serves on the board of directors and is part owner of Bronner Brothers Manufacturing Company, a multi-million dollar family-owned corporation that has been in the hair-care business for over sixty years. In addition, Dr. Bronner is a member of the board of directors of Dr. John Maxwell's training organization, EQUIP. His passion is developing leadership and motivating them for the next level of success. He is a practical strategist with proven techniques for problem solving and conflict resolution. An international teacher, he has traveled to dozens of countries around the globe.

Currently, Dr. Bronner is the founder/senior pastor of Word Of Faith Family Worship Cathedral, an interdenominational ministry, founded in 1991, thriving with more than 15,000 members. He is the author of the books, *Get A Grip*, *Guard Your Gates*, *A Check Up From the Neck Up*, *Treasure Your Silent Years*, *Home Remedies*, *Pass the Baton* and a contributing writer for the books, *Man Power* and *Failure: The Womb of Success.*

Dr. Bronner resides in Atlanta with his wife, Nina, his four daughters and son. Dr. Bronner lives by the adage, "No amount of success can compensate for failure at home."

For further information on
Dr. Dale Carnegie Bronner
please visit
www.dalebronner.com
or write to
Word of Faith Family Worship Cathedral
212 Riverside Parkway
Austell, GA 30168

Leadership Resources
by Samuel R. Chand

FUTURING:
Leading Your Church into Tomorrow

The message will never change. But the methods to present the message can and must change to reach a realm of churchgoers.

Forty-four specific areas that are changing in the church today.

WHO'S HOLDING YOUR LADDER?
Leadership's Most Critical Decision—
Selecting Your Leaders

Those around you, not you, the visionary, will determine your success.

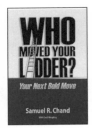

WHO MOVED YOUR LADDER?
Your Next Bold Move

> *Taking the next bold move is not easy—but you finally admit, "I have no choice. I have to jump!" This book will equip you for that leap.*

WHAT'S SHAKIN' YOUR LADDER?
15 Challenges All Leaders Face

> *Take an in-depth look at the common challenges that all leaders face, and benefit from practical advice on facing and overcoming the things that are blocking you from being the best you can be.*

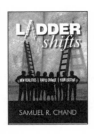

LADDER SHIFTS:
New Realities - Rapid Change - Your Destiny

> *No leader is immune to the shifting circumstances and events that can challenge or stymie their professional or organizational progress. Advance warning of these oncoming storms, together with adequate preparation, can mean the difference between disaster and success.*

LADDER FOCUS:
Creating, sustaining, and enlarging your big picture

> *How to realize your organizational vision by illuminating the many necessary structural and procedural components. It includes easy-to-follow blend of principles, examples, and practical tips to equip you in ensuring the success of your organization.*

CHANGE:
Leading Change Effectively

- *Healthy confessions for those leading change*
- *Tradition and traditionalism*
- *Responding to seasons and times*
- *Levels of change*
- *Factors that facilitate or hinder change*
- *Steps for positive change*
- *Selling your idea*
- *Creating a team*
- *Personal challenges of the leader leading change*

DEVELOPING A LEADERSHIP CULTURE

- *Why do leaders do what they do?*
- *Why and when leaders make changes?*
- *Vision levels of people*
- *Contemporary leadership*
- *Why leaders fail*
- *Qualities of a successful leader*

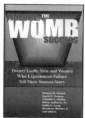

FAILURE:
The Womb of Success

- *Failure is an event not a person*
- *Failure is never final*
- *Twenty leaders tell their stories*

FORMATION OF A LEADER

Spiritual Formation
  - *Born to lead*
  - *Security or sabotage*

Skill Formation
  - *The day Moses became a leader*

Strategic Formation
  - *Live the life you were meant to live*
  - *Mentoring: How to invest your life in others*

FUTURING:
Leading Your Church Into Tomorrow

  - *Futuring leadership traits*
  - *Challenges for the 21st century*
  - *How ministry will change in the next 3–7 years*
  - *Motivational fuels for 21st century church*
  - *Addition versus multiplication of leaders*

12 SUCCESS FACTORS
FOR AN ORGANIZATION

  - *Handling Complexity*
  - *Completion*
  - *Lead and Manage People*
  - *Executional Excellence*

WHAT KEEPS PASTORS UP AT NIGHT

- *Do my people get the vision?*
- *Are things getting done?*
- *How is the team working together?*
- *Do I have the team I need to get it done?*

WHO'S HOLDING YOUR LADDER?

- *Ladder holders determine the Leader's ascent*
- *Selecting your ladder holders*
- *Different ladder holders for different levels*
- *Qualities of a good ladder holder*
- *Development of ladder holders*
- *Leaders versus Managers*
- *Turning ladder holders into ladder climbers*

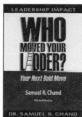

WHO MOVED YOUR LADDER?
Your Next Bold Move

- *What's wrong with me?*
- *What's wrong with my ladder?*
- *What's going on?*
- *What happened to the challenge?*
- *Where's the thrill of achievement?*

UNDERSTANDING PEOPLE:
Managing Conflicts in Your Ministry

- *What conflict does*
- *High maintenance relationships*
- *Predictable times of conflict*
- *Levels of conflict*
- *Diffusing conflict*
- *Conflict resolution*

HOW TO ORDER RESOURCES

WRITE

Samuel R. Chand Consulting
950 Eagles Landing Parkway, Suite 295
Stockbridge, GA 30281

WEBSITE

www.samchand.com

NOTES

1. BULK purchase (10 or more) rates available.

2. Credit cards & checks accepted

Books by
Bishop Dale C. Bronner

Pass the Baton!

"This book contains wisdom that can change your life."

Foreword by John Maxwell

In this important book you will find principles to help people rise to their full potential and become the powerful men and women they are capable of being. You only pass this way once and it would be a tragedy if you failed to take what God has allowed you to experience and invest it in the life of someone who desperately needs what you have to offer.

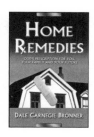

Home Remedies

This book is based on what Abraham—the Father of Nations—taught his children. These inspired principles not only worked in the deserts of Paran but are a practical guide for today. Bishop Bronner tackles the issues that infect and cause sickness in our homes and shares God's prescription for total restoration.

You will find the answers for these and other problems:

- *How can I instill a work ethic in my children?*
- *What is the source of a positive attitude?*
- *How can I help optimize potential in our family?*
- *What is the secret to restoring broken relationships?*

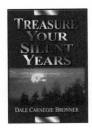

Treasure Your Silent Years

Treasure Your Silent Years will be a vital stepping stone to the destiny God has planned. Quiet times are ordered by God and must be highly prized—they are a treasure the Lord has graciously given. You will discover that the time spent waiting while you are in your silent years is not so much about what you should "do," but what you should "become!"

You will find the answers to these and other questions:

- *Why does the Lord allow us to endure years of silence?*
- *What are the three seasons of life, and how can I prepare for them?*
- *Why does God allow persecution and affliction?*
- *What significant steps should I take when I am hidden behind the scenes?*
- *How will I know when the Lord is ready to release me into my calling?*
- *What lessons will I learn in the silent years?*

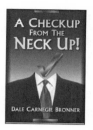

A Checkup from the Neck Up!

In this book you will be given a self-examination that involves your thinking, your speech, your vision, your decision making and much more. You will be asked: What are the strongholds of your life? Can you define your core beliefs? What thoughts dominate your mind? What is the impact of your words? How does your will line up with God's? What is the key to successful decision making? How is your vision? Are the weapons you use carnal or spiritual?

Guard Your Gates!

Your gates are not only a way in—they are a way out! As a child you can probably remember seeing a replica of the three little monkeys—speak no evil, see no evil, hear no evil. In this book you will discover what God's Word says about guarding every area of your life; including how to guard your Mouth, Eye, Mind, Ear, Nose, Flesh, and Heart Gates.

Get a Grip!

Are you someone who could use help to bring your sexual drives under control? Is you weight as unstable as the stock market? Is procrastination the thief of your time? Does depression deprive you of joyous living and meaningful relationship? Do you start off excited about things, but soon discover your interest has waned? Do you live at the mercy of lustful desire and find yourself succumbing to it? Do you lack the discipline and motivation to do what you know you need to do? If the answer to any of these questions is "yes" then "Get A Grip" is the book for you! Here you will find proven strategies for conquering seven of life's most common (but often toughest) problems.

HOW TO ORDER BOOKS BY BISHOP DALE C. BRONNER

WRITE

Word of Faith Family Worship Cathedral
212 Riverside Parkway
Austell, GA 30168

WEBSITE

www.dalebronner.com

NOTES

1. BULK purchase (10 or more) rates available.

2. Credit cards & checks accepted